W9-CEJ-475

THE **Aliveness** FACTOR

THE Aliveness FACTOR

*A Mediterranean Guide
to Joyful Living*

JUAN M. MARTÍN MENÉNDEZ

M·J

NEW YORK

THE **Aliveness** FACTOR
A Mediterranean Guide to Joyful Living

Published in New York, New York, by Morgan James Publishing. Morgan James and The Entrepreneurial Publisher are trademarks of Morgan James, LLC.
www.MorganJamesPublishing.com

The Morgan James Speakers Group can bring authors to your live event. For more information or to book an event visit The Morgan James Speakers Group at www.TheMorganJamesSpeakersGroup.com.

FREE eBook edition for your existing eReader with purchase

PRINT NAME ABOVE

For more information, instructions, restrictions, and to register your copy, go to **www.bitlit.ca/readers/register** or use your QR Reader to scan the barcode:

ISBN 978-1-61448-725-8 paperback
ISBN 978-1-61448-726-5 eBook
ISBN 978-1-61448-727-2 audio
ISBN 978-1-61448-966-5 hardcover
Library of Congress Control Number:
2013949922

Cover Design by:
Bernadette
bskok@ptd.net

Interior Design by:
Bonnie Bushman
bonnie@caboodlegraphics.com

In an effort to support local communities, raise awareness and funds, Morgan James Publishing donates a percentage of all book sales for the life of each book to Habitat for Humanity Peninsula and Greater Williamsburg.

Get involved today, visit
www.MorganJamesBuilds.com

Habitat for Humanity®
Peninsula and
Greater Williamsburg
Building Partner

For my family

Contents

Preface

In the summer of 2010, I was meditating in the sanctuary of a retreat center located on the west coast of Canada, in British Columbia. I had gone there as part of a series of trips I was doing that year to different retreat centers in the world to see them and what they were doing. That afternoon I had been reflecting on what to do next in my life; I felt I was coming to the end of a stage and was unsure what to do. In this uncertainty, and feeling the anxiety of the doubt, I decided to go meditate and ask for guidance. A few years ago, this never would've occurred to me, but now I know that there is a deeper layer of wisdom inside of us that we can access and count on to make important decisions. I sat on a cushion, crossed my legs, and went inside with the question "What do I do next?" After a while, my mind calmed, and I began feeling serene and at peace. I was focusing on my breath, as I had been taught in some meditation classes I had attended, from time to time bringing to my consciousness the question "What do I do next?" I don't know how much time passed, maybe half an hour, and then suddenly, in the space of my consciousness, the answer appeared: *Write, write, write.*

I was intrigued; this was not the kind of answer I expected. Writing had never been on my radar screen. Certainly by then, I was used to listening carefully to my inner wisdom and following it. The very act of being in a place like that and meditating would have been unthinkable for me ten years before. My life had gone through a major transformation after I left my corporate executive career and engaged in a journey of personal search and discovery. So here I was, on the other side of the world from my home base in Spain, being guided by my inner wisdom to write—something I had never done before. But write about what?

The reason I was in that place was because I had the dream of creating resorts where people could grow, expand, and feel the joy of being alive. In my own journey, I had been in quite a few places that had helped me transform my life for good, and I had the desire to facilitate for other people learning experiences like the ones I had had. Every time I talked to others about this dream, I said, "I want to create places for people to come alive and experience the joy of being alive." Aliveness was my passion. Since I am from the Mediterranean, this may seem normal because the Mediterranean cultures are so lively, but the aliveness I was talking about had more nuances to it. In my search, I had discovered dimensions of experience and of our being that play a crucial role in our aliveness and, ultimately, in our joy of living and fulfillment. My inner wisdom didn't tell me what to write about, but I knew it; I had to write about aliveness.

Are we alive just because we breathe?

Are we alive just because our hearts beat?

Are we alive just because we get up every day, do our work, and take care of our responsibilities?

Well, yes, those are good signs that we are alive, especially when compared with the residents of a graveyard. But is this all there is to our aliveness?

Is being vital and energetic the same as being exhausted?

Is being passionate the same as being bored and apathetic?

Is being joyful the same as being numb?

Is being who we really are the same as drowning ourselves?

I know I am beginning this book with a lot of questions, but I believe they will give you an idea of what I mean by *aliveness*. When we are vital, we are more alive. When we are passionate and joyful, we are more alive. When we are who we really are, we are more alive. This is so because our being is more vibrant, and thus we experience *the joy of being alive*.

We all want to be happy, but what is happiness about? Is it not about the joy of living? We may seek happiness by pursuing the different things we want—money, a career, a lifestyle, and so on—but do we not ultimately pursue these things because we want to experience the joy of living? And this joy of living is not just a function of getting all that we want. This is proved by the experience of many people who, having got all that they wanted, don't feel fulfilled and joyful in their lives.

It is my experience that our joy of living comes primarily from our being and feeling vibrant and alive. The joy of living that is so idiosyncratic of the Mediterranean cultures is very much related to this kind of aliveness I am talking about, to what I call *"the Aliveness Factor."*

So, attending to that inner voice that prompted me to write, I have written this book. I have written it to help others be and feel vibrantly alive and experience the joy of living that they want and deserve. My journey provided me with knowledge and insights that I want to pass on to others. Also, I want to share with other people around the world the gifts and the wisdom of my Mediterranean culture when it comes to aliveness and the joy of living.

I have divided the book into three parts. The first part is devoted to the insights I have gained. Here I tell you about my own journey and what I learned about happiness, fulfillment, and aliveness. I go into certain detail because I believe it can inspire others to listen to life's invitations and jump into the unknown, trusting that behind the veil can lie new possibilities and the highs of the joy of living. In this part, I also present the principles that underlie a vibrant aliveness, and show you how most of them are ingrained in the Mediterranean culture's ways of living, providing their peoples with a cultural framework that brings aliveness and joy of living into their lives.

This book is intended to be a self-help book, so part two is devoted to presenting a practical method I have devised to help others be and feel vibrantly alive, and live joyful and highly fulfilling lives.

As in any endeavor, in this one there are challenges to be faced. These may come from our life situation, but they also may come from inside ourselves. Part three is dedicated to showing how to overcome the most important challenges we face in any personal transformation, and to igniting the move toward a vibrant and joyful life.

It is my belief that it is our birthright to experience the joy of being alive, and this book is a tribute and a contribution to it.

Let's begin our journey.

PART I

INSIGHTS

CHAPTER ONE

An Unplanned Journey

June 15, 1999. This date will remain forever in my memory as the day my destiny changed.

Sitting in a meeting room at the Madrid office of the international law firm Baker & McKenzie, I signed the termination agreement from the job I had held for the previous three years.

The lawyer was going through all the points in the agreement before giving it to me for signing. Since I already knew them, my mind wandered into the past, bringing up memories of those three years. No, I didn't feel resentment or sadness as a result of being fired from a job that gave me the status of a successful man. What I felt was relief.

Three years before, I had become country manager for Spain and Portugal of a multinational company in the telecommunications industry, and with it my college dreams had come true. I had become the business executive I had dreamed I would be. But it seemed that life had something different in store for me.

Two weeks before this meeting with the lawyers, I had received a call from our United Kingdom office. It was my boss. He wanted to discuss a few details of a meeting that we had later that week with a customer in Barcelona.

"Are you going to stay overnight?" he asked me.

"No, I am planning to come back to Madrid after the meeting."

"Please, stay, I have to talk to you, and we could do it over dinner."

"Okay," I said, "I will rearrange my schedule for the next day."

He had become the new European CEO the previous month, arriving from the central headquarters in Canada, and he was working on redesigning the business operations.

At a certain moment in that dinner, he told me his new plans for the region: "I want to centralize as much as possible in the UK headquarters."

"What do you want to do with the Spanish office?" I asked, intuiting the answer.

"I just want to have a sales engineer to manage the relationship with the customers. All the rest will be managed from the UK. This will lower the overhead cost and streamline the operations. This means we don't need you anymore."

He was direct and to the point. I was being invited to leave. But the most interesting thing was that I didn't care. After all the initial excitement that I had when I began in this job, I had grown more and more bored and unsatisfied. I didn't have any kind of hard feelings for being fired and thrown out of the kingdom. I had a very good résumé (what we call a curriculum vitae) and saw this as an opportunity to get into a new job where I could feel enthusiasm and motivation again. What I didn't know at the time was that what I longed for was not to be provided by a new job, as I had thought.

That day—June 15, 1999—I began a journey that would transform me and my life in a way that was impossible for me to see at the time. But let's begin at the beginning.

Achieving the Dream

The day I got my degree in telecommunications engineering, I was filled with excitement about the future. I wanted to become a corporate executive and live the life of a successful man. Unlike most of my classmates, who applied for more technical positions, I applied for business-related ones, and sure enough, I ended up in the marketing department of a telecommunications company. One day, as I was watching a TV series at home, there was a scene of a meeting in an office situated in one of the fanciest office buildings in Madrid, which had a Porsche sports car dealership on the ground floor. I remember wishing I were a businessman, had an office like that, and drove a Porsche.

It is said that when we wish something with all of our heart, life maneuvers to make our dream come true. And this is exactly what happened to me. A few years later, I had a fancy office on the eighteenth floor of that same building that I saw in the TV series, I was a corporate executive, and in the garage of the building, I had a shiny new top-of-the-line sporty BMW. When I was offered the position of country manager for Spain and Portugal of a Canadian telecommunications technology manufacturer, a new life opened up for me, the life of the corporate executive I had wished to be.

But something must have been missing, because after the excitement I felt at the beginning had faded, gradually I became more and more bored, disengaged, and dissatisfied. I wish at that point I had read Stephen Covey's book *The Seven Habits of Highly Effective People*, especially where he says, "Sometimes we climb the ladder only to find out when we arrive that it is leaning against the wrong wall."

Mr. Covey's insight might have made me think on such questions as: Is this the case for me? Is this my place? Am I selling my soul for an image of success? Whose expectations am I living for?

But I hadn't read the book yet. I imagine that even if I had read it at that time, I wouldn't have been able to grasp the deep meaning of these questions. I needed to go through certain experiences before in order to be ready for them. As the saying goes, "When the student is ready, the master appears." And this student was not yet ready.

The Call to Adventure

It seems that life sometimes gives us what we need the most even if we don't see and fully understand it at the moment.

What I needed was a shake-up that would remove me from my comfort zone and oblige me to take a deeper look into my life. And this shake-up came in the form of the loss of my job. This not only relieved me from my daily activities and responsibilities; it also opened up the possibilities for exploring other aspects of life and of myself.

I wasn't worried about getting another job. I knew that I had a very good professional profile and that it wouldn't be difficult to find a good job. I made my résumé and sent it to the major headhunters. Then I got ready to enjoy my time off.

Being single and with no family responsibilities, I was free to do whatever I wanted, and I decided to do a trip to Peru. But instead of taking a travel agency package, I felt like doing something more adventurous, and just bought a plane ticket to Lima with no plans made in advance.

I was traveling alone and decided on the spot where to go. I traveled all over the country. I trekked the Andes to reach the Machu Picchu Inca ruins. I got into the jungle navigating the Amazon River, and I spent time in little villages with local people. All these experiences connected me with a sense of adventure that I loved and that made me feel so alive. All of a sudden, life had become exciting, interesting, a discovery, and an adventure. One morning I arrived at Machu Picchu after four days of tough trekking in the Andes. I had been following the Camino del Inca, a trail that goes to the ruins, and suddenly, after a turn in the trail, I was faced with one of the most beautiful images I had seen. Before me, down in a green valley, appeared the ruins that I had seen so many times in pictures and on television. I sat for a while, letting the image sink in me and feeling the sense of awe that invaded my soul. I contemplated the remains of this civilization, wondering how they would have lived and thinking how interesting life is, how lucky I was for being able to see that, and how much I had lost the sense of adventure I loved so much in my childhood and teenage years. I was so invaded by the emotion that tears came to my eyes.

That night, in the comfort of a hotel bed, I missed the sense of wonder and adventure I had experienced the previous four nights sleeping less comfortably in a tent in the middle of the Andes. I realized how much this trip was nourishing and enlivening me at the depths of my soul. My soul craved new experiences, change, and discovery, and it had been dying in the routine I had fallen into.

I spent a whole month in Peru, and when I came back to Spain, I felt renewed in my soul.

On my return from this trip, I began having interviews with headhunters. Interestingly enough, I wanted a job similar to the one I had left behind. Having my expenses covered by my savings, I could afford to wait until a good opportunity emerged, so I decided not to hurry but to take my time.

A few years before, I had begun reading books on spirituality, philosophy, and psychology out of an interest in the deeper aspects and questions of life. Now that I had time, I went deeper into this and found myself more and more engaged in and fascinated with what I was discovering. Something in me resonated with all of that and was hungry for it. Being an engineer with a very educated mind, I was not the kind of *woo-woo* guy who accepted everything without rational and critical consideration. However, my mind was open to the new.

Nearly without my realizing it, a year had passed, and I decided it was time to get back to work. I had had my sabbatical year, so to speak, and I had to return to the working life. I began to be more active in my job search, and one day, what seemed to be the very thing I was looking for appeared in front of me, on my computer screen.

Searching the offers that companies looking for executives had placed on the website of the business school where I had studied, I found one that immediately caught my attention:

country manager of an Internet start-up company. It was what I was looking for, and . . . it was the Internet—the magical word, the booming industry at the time, the fanciest place to be in the information technology industry. Within minutes, I sent my résumé to apply for the position.

In a matter of days, the company answered and asked me to travel to London for an interview, where I met with the company founders. They were in the early stages of a very ambitious project. Big names in the technology field were backing it, and an American venture capital firm had agreed to invest $25 million as a first round of financing. The interview went so well that right there, they made me an offer to come on board and become the executive to develop the business in Spain and Portugal.

I had gotten it! I had gotten another dream job. This company had a great future ahead, and I was going to be at the top. Moneywise? I was going to have stock options in a company that was intended to go public within one or two years. Being aware of the incredible valuations that Internet companies were reaching in the stock market, I was sure I was set to become a millionaire within a few years. The contract was going to be sent to me the following week for me to sign. I felt I was living one of the stories I used to read in *Fortune* magazine, and I could hardly keep still in my seat on the flight back to Madrid.

But instead of the contract, what I received one week later was a call from the CEO telling me that the venture capital company had decided at the last minute to back out. He asked me to wait because they thought they could find another investor within a matter of weeks. They couldn't, and the project was finally abandoned.

After this I began to wonder if the universe didn't want me to return to my former life. During the year, among the executive positions I had been presented by headhunters, there were another two that I was really interested in and excited about, that I had been the selected candidate for, and that, due to unexpected last-minute changes, vanished. Could it be that the universe was trying to tell me that I had to look in another direction? The books I was reading talked about the soul's journey, about the deeper dynamics of life, and about the purpose of our lives. Could it be that the purpose of my life was in a different direction? If not, I was having really weird bad luck.

Three months after this disappointment, I made the decision that would change my life path forever; I decided to stop looking for a job and take my destiny into my own hands.

Life Sometimes Turns in Unexpected Ways

Start my own company—that was what I was going to do. I had wanted to become an entrepreneur since my years in the university, and it seemed that life had put me in a position to go for it. But what kind of business should I start? I had no clue. My natural industry was telecommunications, but I couldn't see what kind of business I could start.

I began talking to some of my contacts to find out about possible opportunities. One day, I met with a former client in a cafeteria for an informal conversation. Many times before, we had sat together in meeting rooms or restaurants to talk about business, but that day, he was a friend whose advice I needed.

"You look relaxed," he began.

"Oh, yes, I feel more serene and happy."

"You said when we talked on the phone that you have decided to start up your own company."

"Yes," I said, "it's something that I have always wanted to do, and I think that now is a good moment to go for it."

As I said this, I realized how little enthusiasm I felt about what I was saying. I paused and took a sip of my spicy herbal tea; its smell brought to me images of southeast Asia, and I felt a rush of excitement and emotion.

"What are you thinking of?" he continued.

"I have no idea. I am trying to figure out something in the information technology and telecommunications industry."

"Are you in a hurry?" he asked.

"I've been out of work for a year now, and I want to get back as soon as possible."

"If you want to get started quickly, go into representing commercially here the products of a foreign technology manufacturer. I can give you some contacts."

"No," I said, "I don't want that."

I knew I didn't want to go back to selling technology. I was thinking of something more motivating for me, of creating a project that used technology, especially in the Internet field.

I focused my research in this direction and started planning a trip to the United States, to places like Silicon Valley and Stanford University, to see technology trends and identify possible business ideas. When I told a friend about my plans, she said: "If you start up a business like that, you are going to end up doing the same things that you have been doing so far and that you say you don't feel any enthusiasm or passion for. If you are going to California, why don't you go to a place called Esalen Institute and have a look? Knowing you and your interests, I am sure you will enjoy it very much."

So I went to the Esalen website to learn more about the place, and I felt immediately engaged. Terms such as "human potential," "consciousness evolution," "sensory awareness," and "wisdom of the body" got me excited. I felt a rush of energy in my body. Yes, I wanted to go there. Everything sounded so interesting! It resonated with my passion for the depths of life and human experience.

Esalen is an institute devoted to human and social development and transformation. It started in the 1960s as the pioneer in this field in North America. Today it is a world-class institute that offers more than five hundred workshops a year in a wide range of fields.

I decided to change my plans. Instead of doing a work-related trip, I designed a new and more adventurous one to explore who I was and to learn about those topics about which I had become more and more passionate. I thought that in the future, I might not be able to have the free time to do it.

In planning my travels, I had learned also about two other centers that seemed very interesting: Findhorn in northern Scotland and Omega in Rhinebeck, New York, institutions that were, together with Esalen, pioneers in the field of holistic education. So I arranged plans for a three-month trip to go and attend in each of these places the personal growth programs for which they were so well-known.

I was really excited about this trip, which was a big contrast with my lack of excitement for the business trip I was planning before. My first stop on this adventure would be northern Scotland.

Findhorn: Connecting from the Heart

Findhorn is a spiritual community, an ecovillage, and an international center for holistic education. They offer a wide range of programs for personal exploration and growth as well as for the development of sustainable ways of living, programs that are attended by people from all over the world.

The day I arrived at Cluny Hill College, a former Victorian hotel turned into an educational facility, I felt the kindness of the place; the person behind the reception counter seemed to have the radiance of happiness in her face. She welcomed me kindly, but it felt different from the type of kind welcome I was accustomed to in hotels. There was something else here. There was more heart—it wasn't just manners.

I had registered for two of Findhorn's signature programs—Experience Week and Life Purpose—and felt the expectation of the experiences that were in store for me in the following weeks. Experience Week is a program for people to experience what Findhorn is about and to learn the spiritual and community principles that are at its core. The Life Purpose is a program intended to help participants get in touch with their deepest selves, their hearts' longings, and a sense of their purpose in life.

A little while after registering and taking my luggage to my room, I found myself sitting in a circle with some twenty other strangers and listening to a short introduction of the Experience Week program made by two members of the community who identified themselves as "focalizers." During the week, we were going to have different activities from group meetings, presentations by community members, outdoor activities, and games. We also would be working a few mornings in a department to experience how the folks there approach work. It seemed it was going to be a very busy week, and certainly it was that and much more.

After this introduction, we moved to a bigger room to do what they call "group discovery games." And that's what we did; we played games, as children do. So there I was, playing like a kid with strangers, some younger than I, and others older, who had come from various countries in the world. The amazing thing was that after an hour and a half, we were not strangers anymore; the atmosphere was filled with joy, friendship, and kindness, and all in less than two hours while playing children's games!

This seemed to me certain proof that at Findhorn, they knew about the human heart and relationships. During the week, I sensed that I had arrived there with armor around my heart, and now I felt it was melting; I found myself hugging others, with warm feelings toward them, and sharing from my heart.

As the focalizers said in their introduction, the week was filled with experiences and discoveries, but the most important one for me was the discovery of my heart in relating to others and the real meaning of human connection. Before I realized it, the week was over—but the embers of it still remain very alive within me to this day. The last day when most of the group members were about to leave, I felt in my heart the sadness and pain of separation that we normally feel when leaving those with whom we have deep heart connections. The difference was that I had met these people only one week before. I knew that I would never see most of them again but that the time spent with them in the spirit of love and human connection would remain with me for the rest of my life.

The following week, I began the Life Purpose program, still feeling the glow of Experience Week within me. This time I was to explore the deepest dimensions of myself in search of my soul and that for which I was longing deep inside me. All the ideas—about the inner self, the soul, and the spiritual dimension of human beings—were not strange to me because I had read so much about them. But the difference was that this program was not about ideas, but about *experiences*. It was about actually coming inside oneself and connecting with that dimension. Just as when I began reading books on spirituality and consciousness, there was a part of me that felt at home with all this. During the week, we engaged in various exercises that helped me to experience what I knew in theory and get a sense of the spiritual dimension of life and of my being. I also discovered meditation.

Every morning I would get up at six to go to the sanctuary and meditate. I loved this place. There were no images of gods or saints, or any other religious beings, just a few chairs and pillows arranged in a circle around a bouquet of fresh flowers with a candle in the middle. The peace of the place was amazing, and it imbued me with an inner silence and sense of the sacred that renewed and nurtured me in the deepest depths of my being.

At the end of the week, I didn't have more clarity on my professional career, as had been my intention when I signed up for this program, but I was clear about something more important: I found that my soul was craving the feeling of emotion and a sense of adventure, and maybe the purpose of my life had to do with those cravings. We are very used to thinking of the purpose of our lives in terms of the work we do, but I learned that the purpose of life is a much broader thing. It has to do with the longings and deep motivations of our hearts, which, from a spiritual understanding of life, is our soul's message of what it needs and wants to experience.

Esalen: Being in the Body

My experiences at Findhorn had left me with a sense of the spiritual dimension of life and the satisfaction that comes from feeling the heart and connecting with others. When I left there, I felt uplifted in my spirit and ready for the next stage of my journey, which was going to take place on the other side of the Atlantic, in California, at Esalen Institute.

Among its various programs, Esalen offers one called the WorkStudy. This is a monthlong program that is intended to provide an extended experience of personal growth and exploration through the experience of daily life as part of its staff and through classes on a certain personal growth topic. The idea is to provide participants with the environment and structure for them to explore themselves and grow as human beings.

On a Sunday afternoon, I set foot on the Esalen property after a four-hour trip from San Francisco. The beauty of the land was breathtaking. Situated on the cliffs of Big Sur, this place felt to me like fresh air.

Just after arrival, all the participants in the WorkStudy program gathered and sat in a circle for an introductory session. The person leading it began by asking us to close our eyes, withdraw attention from the outside, and place it inside, on whatever we were feeling at the moment, to get out of our heads and get into our real experience. This was the prelude to a month in which I was going to discover my body and the delicious sense of aliveness that it is capable of providing.

The next morning, I walked one and a half miles from the staff complex to the main property, where I had to be at seven thirty for my training. After the night's sleep, I felt rested and ready for whatever the day ahead had in store for me. Putting in practice what I had experienced the day before, I walked slowly, letting myself be imbued by the experience. I breathed in the fresh air of the morning, which brought the smells of the ocean mixed with that of the redwoods. The bird's noises mixed with those coming from the waves splashing on the cliffs, and together they sounded like a morning dance. The fog over the water framed by the cliffs that fell sharply to the ocean painted before my eyes a picture of wonder and awe. I felt so good that my mind didn't even think about what was going to happen that day. I just enjoyed the walk and the experience I was having.

My work for the month was going to be lodge keeper; I had to take care that everything in the dining lodge was okay and give a hand in the kitchen. All of a sudden, I, the former corporate executive, the guy who wanted to be rich and at the top, found myself filling coffee machines, cleaning tables, or chopping vegetables. And the most interesting thing is that I was paying to do this! But everything had its reason.

That very first day was filled with new learning—how to fill the coffee machine, where the bread was, how to organize the salad bar—but also with the rewards of discovering the gestalt awareness practice.

Gestalt is at the core of Esalen. It is both a practice of contact with the experience of the present moment that enhances the experience itself, and a therapeutic approach that focuses on the integration of the person to become more whole and hence feel a greater fullness of being. In the process of living, we tend to lose parts of ourselves, like our capacity to feel, for example, or to repress parts of our personality that we don't accept. When these parts are reintegrated and experienced, the natural outcome is a more integrated person and a higher plenitude of life.

As work scholars, we were told to pay attention during our work to whatever feelings might arise in us due to the activity itself and through the interaction with others. I began to become aware of my emotional reactions to the different situations that I would find myself in during my shift. For example, if someone would tell me that I had forgotten to fill the coffee machine, I became aware of the feeling of fear that roused in me, the fear of being punished, of being rejected. It's not that this was going to happen, but this was my emotional reaction. Or I would have to organize the dining tables on the deck overlooking the ocean, and while doing that, I became aware of a feeling of expansion and playfulness.

Esalen offers a wide range of activities to its guests and staff, and among these offerings are movement classes. I decided to try one the next morning before getting to work, and I fell in love with it.

I got up early, like the day before, and walked to the main property. Again, the experience was deeply rewarding. The morning movement class was at 8 A.M. in a conference room they call Huxley, from whose glass wall I could see the beautiful cliffs of Big Sur. There were some thirty people in the room, wearing comfortable clothes and barefoot. We started by doing some stretches to wake up our bodies and then began to move to the rhythm of music. I had always loved music and dance, but this was different. The class leader encouraged us to move and dance, focusing on feeling our bodies and giving them the freedom to express whatever we were feeling, to be playful and creative, to interact and play with others if we felt like it. At the beginning, I felt shy, and I moved in a very controlled way, but as the class went by, I sort of loosened up and moved more freely. I just loved it. I felt free, connected, playful, and alive. It was not just dance; it was freedom. It was connection. It was release. By the end of the class, everybody's spirit was uplifted, which showed in our smiling and luminous faces. With this spirit, I went to work, and it literally changed my day. I decided to include this class in my daily activities.

The theme of that month's educational program for work scholars was Gestalt Process. Four evenings a week, we had a class to learn about processing our feelings and emotions so that we could grow and become more whole. The class was not what we normally imagine when we think of a class: a room filled with tables, a board, and a teacher to give a lecture. No, we gathered in a room with no tables, only pillows on the floor where we sat. And there was no lecture. It was everything experiential; we were going to learn by experience. The lecturer was not a lecturer either, but a specialist in gestalt therapy who was going to work with us to show what gestalt therapy was about and to help us in our growth.

In these classes, I became aware of how disconnected I was from my feelings and body, from real experience, and how much I lived in my head.

After the first week, I felt different, more connected with myself, more alive and happier. Certainly, Esalen, like Findhorn, was not an ordinary place, but it wasn't a far-out place either; most of the work scholars were people like me, professionals either spending their vacations there or on a sort of life transition journey.

Being an engineer and coming from the corporate world, I was very used to working with my mind, to living in my mind, so to speak; in this place, I rediscovered my body and my feelings and experienced a heightened sense of aliveness. The same way that my adventure in Peru enlivened my soul and the experiences at Findhorn enlivened my heart, what I was experiencing in this place enlivened my body and feelings.

Esalen has amazing natural hot springs, and they became another very important part of my month there. A few years before, the El Niño storms had taken away the old baths. Temporary ones had been built, and they sat on platforms that hung, seemingly suspended in midair, off the cliffs overlooking the Pacific Ocean. I spent hours and hours sitting in these temporary wooden tubs filled with mineral waters, blown away by the beauty of the sight before me. These sessions became a kind of meditation for me, moments when I felt connected with the wholeness of life, moments of awe and wonder at the beauty of life and nature. It seemed that I was able to appreciate the exquisiteness of life for its own sake for the first time.

The month went very quickly, and before I realized it, it was over. I had to leave and continue my personal exploration adventure, which would take me to the East Coast of the United States, to the Omega Institute.

Omega: The Work I Love

Located in Rhinebeck in the state of New York, Omega is another of the holistic education places that began in the 1960s to provide a venue for people to explore and learn about the depths of life and wisdom traditions of the world. I had decided to explore the topic of my vocation in this place. It was clear that my corporate executive job hadn't fulfilled me. I had achieved what I wanted and what I had dreamed of since my college years, but I hadn't felt the fulfillment or the happiness that I longed for. So I decided to register for two programs at Omega: Creating the Work You Love, and Creativity and Self-Expression.

I had never thought about vocation in the terms I discovered in these programs. The main idea presented was the importance of aligning what we do in our external life—in this case, the work we do—with who we are inside. Although the framework used was holistic, what the program stressed was the importance of staying open and aware of the urges that motivate us and connect us to our passions. And here is where my questioning began: What was I passionate about? I had no clue. After my teenage love for electronics, I had never again felt any passion or strong interest for anything. So when I was faced with the question, I didn't know what to answer.

In these workshops, work was presented from a different perspective than how I and many others had always understood it. Work was presented as a way of self-expression. Usually, work is seen more in terms of earning our living, getting the money we want, or building a career and a position. But what about the heart? What about the soul? Is work only a means to an end?

I learned that doing something you love and care for is very important when it comes to feeling fulfilled and satisfied with the work you do. But it is equally important with regard to your feeling deeply alive. When you love what you do or you care deeply about it, your heart and soul are very alive because they are engaged and activated. The outer and the inner are in alignment.

It was clear that if I wanted to feel fulfillment and satisfaction at work, I needed to find this alignment, which was very much related to identifying what I really loved. At the Life Purpose program at Findhorn, I had realized that my soul craved feeling, emotion, and adventure. At Esalen, I had experienced being in the body, expression, music, flow, and play, and I loved these too. Also, I had my interest in—passion for, I should say—the field of wisdom, consciousness, spirituality, personal growth, and the depths of life. These were very important clues to where my heart was and the direction in which I could find the vibrancy I lacked in my previous job. But it is one thing to gain some insights into our inner selves and another to translate those into our actual lives.

When I left Omega, I felt the challenge ahead of me. I had lived life-changing experiences on my trip, learned important facts about life, and gained self-knowledge. Now it was time to come home and face the reality of getting back to work after this sabbatical period. I knew it wasn't going to be easy. I was different; all the experiences I had lived had taught me key lessons, but most importantly, they had transformed me, my values, and how I saw life and my life. This meant I couldn't go back to the past; I only could go ahead, into the future—a future I could not see, but one that I wanted to be filled with the feeling of aliveness that I had experienced.

The Guidance of Life

What should I do now? This was the question in my head when I landed at Madrid-Barajas Airport after an eight-hour flight from New York.

Prior to leaving home three months before, I had made the decision to start up a business in the field of information technology, an idea I had come to not out of love, passion, or enthusiasm, but out of pragmatism. But the person who came back from this trip was different from the one who departed, and this new me had to review the decisions I had made before I left.

Should I stick with my plans to start up a business project my heart was clearly not in? If not, what else could I do?

I didn't feel the motivation and the drive to keep on track with my former plan, and this new me didn't think it was the right thing to do for my life happiness, fulfillment, and satisfaction. But I didn't see any other possibility.

Once again, something seemed to be working behind the scenes.

A few months before my trip, I had met with a former employee, and he told me that I had to meet a man he had worked for at another company, who had left the executive life and now worked on his own, training corporate executives. He said that we had many things in common and gave me his telephone number, insisting that I call him. I didn't feel too inclined to do so and just forgot about it until one day, weeks later, the idea crossed my mind, and I took the phone and called him.

We agreed to meet for a beer and have a chat. He told me about the change he had made in his life and how happy he now was, talking to people and sharing his experience with other executives to help them in their work. It was clear that he was a happy man; his eyes and his voice were vibrant, and he seemed passionate about what he was doing. I thought it was a nice story, and that was all.

But when I came back from my trip and was dealing with my dilemma, I remembered his story, though this time I saw it with different eyes. After all the workshops and programs I had participated in during my trip, I knew that I very much enjoyed being in groups, connecting with people, and learning about personal growth. Could this possibly be the work for me? I had been in the corporate world and knew its dynamics, needs, and problems. I was an insider. Why not consider moving into corporate training?

This would be a big change in career, but most importantly, it would be a change of the identity I had built for myself as a business executive. Since my youth, I had been building this identity and this dream. So now I was faced with a bigger dilemma than changing careers. I was faced with the dilemma of whether to keep my old identity and dream, or build new ones. The latter would mean letting go of the past and embracing a new me, a new life, and a new destiny.

The meeting of this ex-executive-turned-corporate-trainer had opened for me a possibility that I would never have thought about. It looked like the universe was gently taking me by the hand in a new direction.

After some time of consideration and an inner battle among the different forces inside me, I made the decision to abandon the past and embrace a new future that promised to be more rewarding and fulfilling for me. I decided to focus my search on getting into corporate training and pursuing my new passion for the fields of personal growth, spirituality, and expression.

Estudio 3: The Artist in Me

Since I had enjoyed the morning movement classes at Esalen so much and had felt so alive in them, when I returned to Spain, I began looking for a place where I could find something similar. I found it at Estudio 3, a dance and acting studio located in a lively area of downtown Madrid.

The moment I entered its doors to get some information, I knew that it was a place for me. I felt it; I felt a rush of excitement like when you meet a woman or a man and feel you have fallen in love. And that increased when Ana, the office attendant, began explaining to me all the regular classes Estudio 3 offered: acting, modern dance, expressive movement, voice training, singing, improvisation . . . . Just listening to the possibilities, I felt so excited my heartbeat seemed to be saying, "Yes, yes, yes."

I didn't think twice; I signed up for the acting, dance, voice, and body expression classes. Saying that they were great doesn't tell half the story. I loved them. I found myself fully immersed in the world of expression, art, play, and creativity. I spent most of the afternoons there, moving from one class to the other, not getting tired of it and loving it so much.

Sometimes I could hardly believe it was me doing all that. The former corporate executive, the guy whose original ambition had been to be the CEO of a major company, was there doing all those things, playing, acting, and having such a great time expressing himself freely.

One day, I was doing an improvisation with a classmate, and I decided to play the foolish guy role. I just began telling crazy things, jumping from one side of the room to the other fooling her, making faces. That day, we had an audience from the public, and they got into laughing at all that. My improv partner decided to play the game, and we had a lot of fun. It didn't matter there were people watching; we just had fun, and the public had fun with us. When we finished, I thought, *My God, if some people saw me doing this, they wouldn't believe it!*

And it was true; it seemed I was doing something out of character for me. But the truth is, I was actually doing something that was true to who I really was. There was in me a playful boy who loved playing. There was also in me an artist, an actor, a performer who loved being on the stage, expressing his soul and communicating with people. I had never explored this facet of my personality, yet it felt so natural to me.

In Estudio 3, I found something more important than an activity I enjoyed very much. I found a part of my soul. I found a part of me that, when given expression, filled me with joy and life. I had the heart of an artist and the head of an engineer, but the latter had run my life so far. Now the artist had come to the surface and was enriching me in ways I had never imagined. I loved these activities so much that I sometimes said to my classmates, "If I were now twenty years old, I would choose a different career. I would pursue a career in acting, dance, or music."

Estudio 3 became another stage in my personal journey of self-discovery and enlivening. Stage by stage, place by place, experience by experience, I was finding the keys to my life satisfaction and fulfillment. And in the process, I was feeling more and more alive.

But there were still more revelations ahead.

A New Job

After my decision to refocus my work and move into corporate training, I began to look for ways to materialize it. I didn't know how to proceed. My former-executive-turned-corporate-trainer friend had developed his own programs in emotional intelligence and productivity. So, a possibility was to develop a program on a certain subject and offer it to companies. Another route was to join a corporate training consultancy and work for it as an executive trainer.

I was in this consideration when another "chance" event happened. My brother had just attended a training program in leadership that he liked very much. He suggested I talk to the trainer, who also happened to be a partner in the company, to get some advice. I thought it was a good idea and phoned him.

The afternoon we met in his company's offices I was totally open. I told him my story and how I had come to decide to get into executive training. Once again, it seemed I was in the flow. The company executives were looking for senior trainers for their leadership program. They wanted trainers with real experience in leadership positions and in business. He thought I could be a good leadership trainer; I had the real life experience and also the right motivation. After I had some meetings with the other partners, they made an offer for me to join them.

After a period of training and learning the material, the day came when I had to teach my first program. It was a group of managers from a major Spanish bank. I still remember so clearly that very first day. I was so nervous. I had to lead a full day of training, and although I had studied the material, this would be the very first time I was actually doing this kind of work.

My nervousness didn't wait to show up. While I was preparing the material in the room before the group arrived, I began to sweat. The temperature of the room was a little high, but my sweating didn't exactly come from this. It came from my anxiety. Before long, my shirt was soaking wet. Oh my God, what impression was I going to give? I ran to the hotel reception desk to ask for help. They gave me the key to one of the rooms, and I managed to dry my shirt with the hair dryer. So there I was, on my very first day in this kind of work, fifteen minutes before the course was to begin, with my shirt in one hand and a hair dryer in the other. What a beginning!

But I soon forgot it all. The moment I got started, I felt comfortable, and the day went by very well. At the end, when I passed out the evaluation sheet, on a scale of one to ten, all of them gave me nines and tens. I had passed the test, at least my test. I could do this, and do it well.

I felt this work was very natural for me. I had fun, and I enjoyed talking to groups, connecting with people, and sharing things I had learned. I also liked the fact that in one way or another, I could bring some good to their lives. I loved when, at the end of a training program, they said to me things like, "This is going to help me not only in my work, but also in my personal life. Thank you."

Two years later, I created a training company. I wanted to help other companies improve the performance, satisfaction, and well-being of their employees. In the end, I started up my own business, as I had planned when I made the decision to take my destiny into my own hands, but it turned out to be very different from the one I had first envisioned. This one felt more aligned with who I was— and with my own fulfillment and aliveness.

Going Deep into Myself

After my experiences at Esalen, I had grown more and more interested in gestalt and humanistic psychology. I had been told about a school in Madrid that had a very good three-year training program for gestalt therapists, and I decided to embark on this journey. It is not that I wanted to become a therapist; I wanted to learn about me and to better understand human nature. Everything I had heard coincided with the fact that this was a life-changing program.

And it was true. During those three years, I undertook a personal process that took me to know myself in ways that I couldn't have imagined. The approach was essentially experiential.

Once a month, and in a group setting, we met for a whole weekend to work on ourselves as a way to experience and internalize the concepts. Working with the experience of the here and now, I learned where I was blocked, the parts of my personality I had alienated, what I did to avoid contact, and the mechanisms or strategies I had developed in my childhood to face the world that were not serving me anymore.

The power of the program was in the feedback received by the group and by the teacher. We engaged in group dynamics and exercises that brought to the forefront aspects of ourselves that we then gained consciousness of through the feedback received. It was not easy, believe me, to hear what I had to hear sometimes and to say what I had to say sometimes. The agreement was total honesty for the sake of our own growth and benefit. I had never been in an environment so open, risky, and supportive at the same time.

Among the many realizations that I had and the knowledge that I gained in this program, I consider the one about feeling our feelings to be one of the most important ones. In my month at Esalen, I had already begun to grasp the importance of this in relation to our feeling alive, but here I saw that by blocking the flow of feeling, something I did, we disconnect from ourselves and lose a solid sense of self.

When I was forty, right in the middle of life, this program helped me to mature, to become a more integrated, whole, and self-aware person, and prepared me for the second half of my life. I had heard of the midlife crisis as an opportunity for change and transformation for a fulfilling second half of life. What I didn't know was that for me, it was going to mean such a big transformation.

Closing the Circle

As I have been working on this book, some years after that meeting at the offices of Baker & McKenzie, I look back and realize what a journey it has been since then. But most importantly, I realize what a journey it continues to be because today I live life as a journey—and that makes it adventurous, interesting, and exciting.

Little did I know that day what was going to happen. Maybe the universe knew what my destiny was and maneuvered to get me on track. It could be as well that there is no destiny and that we make our lives with the decisions we make along the way. This has been a matter of discussion since we, as a species, began to think and wonder who we are and what this thing we call life is all about. But it wouldn't be fair to leave this very important aspect in ambiguity, not revealing where I stand.

As you can imagine, yes, I believe that there is a higher intelligence at work in life and in our lives. We can use God, Spirit, Tao, Brahman, Yahweh, or any name that man has used over time to refer to ultimate reality. I believe that we are far more than our bodies, minds, and physical lives, that there is a spiritual dimension, and that our lives have meaning and a spiritual purpose. This doesn't mean that we don't have freedom or that our lives are already laid out. I believe that together with the deeper currents active in the depths of our very beings, our will is another powerful force in the shaping of our lives.

But in the end, I think that what really matters is not so much the set of beliefs that we use to interpret our lives and give meaning to what happens in them, but the following of our heart and the listening to our inner wisdom to make the decisions that shape our lives moment by moment, turn by turn. There is a deeper layer of wisdom and intelligence in ourselves beyond what we normally call our minds. We can call this layer our soul, our inner self, or our unconscious mind, but it is real, and we can tap into it and get from there the kind of wisdom that will bring the highest good for us.

In the mythology of all cultures, there is a myth called "the hero's journey." As all myths, it represents an archetypal human story. In this case, it is the story of a person who is invited by life to go on a journey on which he gets transformed, grows, and learns lessons. The journey begins with a call to adventure that normally happens through events that shake his life. Then the person has the choice to accept it or not. If he does, he departs on a journey that takes him through a series of experiences that will transform him and will bring him new learning and new insights. Finally, the hero comes back home and is able to help others with what he has learnt.

Looking at this definition, I can see that I have gone through the hero's journey. By taking away my executive job, life invited me on an adventure. By deciding to follow my heart, I accepted the invitation, and then I embarked on a journey where I have learned about happiness, fulfillment, and aliveness. By prompting me to write this book, my inner wisdom has led me to the final stage of the journey: share with others what I learnt and help them with it. However, I don't think this is the final stage, but the beginning of a new journey. Today, aliveness and the joy of living have become my passion and my mission, and I want to be of service for others and to help them live joyful, vibrant, and highly fulfilling lives.

CHAPTER TWO

What Does It Mean to Be Alive?

Something I had never thought about before going through my life-changing journey was what it really means to be alive. Life was the condition of existence. I breathed; therefore, I was alive. Or, as the French philosopher René Descartes put it, "I think, therefore I exist." However, as I went along the different experiences of my journey, I noticed something: I felt more alive in each and every one of them. It seemed that life wasn't just a matter of black or white, existing or not existing; there were degrees of aliveness. If my Peruvian adventure made me feel more alive, there was something in me that was more alive. If in my time spent sharing with others at Findhorn I felt more alive, there was something in me that was more alive. If in my performances at Estudio 3 I felt more alive, there was something in me that was more alive. Certainly, the definition of "aliveness" that I had needed to be revised.

Today, I understand it differently. I see our aliveness not in biological terms, alive versus dead, but in terms of vibrancy. The more vibrant we are, the more alive we are, and the more alive we feel. It is like light; there are different degrees, from the darkness of the night to the brightness of a sunny day. Translating this into human terms, we could say: from the deadness of boredom and apathy to the aliveness of passion and enthusiasm.

Our aliveness is multidimensional the same way we are multidimensional beings, and a function of how vibrant our bodies, our hearts, and our souls are. The more vibrant we are in all these three dimensions, the more alive we are, and the more we feel the joy of being alive. In the different experiences I had, I felt more alive because I felt more vibrant in one or more of these three dimensions.

My adventure in Peru enlivened my soul. The sense of adventure, of discovery, the living of new experiences made my soul vibrant because one of the needs of our soul is to discover and experience. When we come to the world and are little infants, our natural tendency is to go and discover the world, discover life. But then, as we grow up, we tend to fall into the known and the routine, and to lose that sense of discovery and adventure, and with it vibrancy in our soul. What I learned in Peru is the importance of recapturing that sense of adventure that makes life interesting and exciting if we have lost it, as I had.

The experiences at Findhorn enlivened my heart. The connection with others, the love, and the human warmth made my heart vibrant. Our hearts are our emotional dimension, and the more open and filled with vibrant emotions, such as love, joy, or passion, the more alive they are, and the more alive we are. However, one of the things that life can produce in us is the shutting down of our hearts. Difficult experiences, disappointments, betrayals, and emotional pain of various kinds can make us close down our hearts as a way of protection. However, this comes with a price, the price of diminishing our capacity to experience joy, love, and passion, and with that diminishing our aliveness.

At Esalen, I experienced the enlivening of my body by the movement, expression, and connection with it. When we move our bodies and express ourselves through the movement, they come alive. However, the dynamics of modern life tend to take us to live in our minds, to think, to process information, to talk, disconnecting us from our bodies. In this place, I learned that our bodies are not just the carriers of our minds, but a dimension of our experience and of our being that is as important as any of the other dimensions, and the main source of the delights of the physical world.

The acting classes at Estudio 3 enlivened my spirit. There was an artist in me that was lying dormant, and the moment it awakened, it filled me with aliveness—with *his* aliveness. Deep inside of us, we can have an artist, an explorer, a teacher, a leader, or a healer who sits there dormant, waiting to be awakened. When this happens, we feel a rush of life flowing through us because a part of us comes alive. Our spirit is our inner self, and it is much larger than our outer personality. The more we give it expression, the more alive it is, and the more alive we are at the soul dimension.

Together with my feeling more alive, another feeling that was common to all these experiences was joy; in all of these places, I felt joyful and happy. The vibrancy of my body, of my heart, and of my soul filled me with joy and made life and living a delight. I literally experienced the joy of being alive, and realized that the happiness and fulfillment that we all seek is much more a function of this vibrancy than of all the external things where we tend to try to find it, be it money, a career, our lifestyle, or something else.

All of these may help; they are factors of our happiness and joy of living, but my exploration of human nature and my Mediterranean background have taught me that the biggest factor of all is the Aliveness Factor.

Being from the Mediterranean, I already had that wisdom in my cultural DNA, but I had to go through all those experiences to consciously realize this truth. As usually happens, I had never taken the time to have a deeper look at my own culture and the wisdom inherent in it. But the release from my daily responsibilities that came with the loss of my job, and the exploration of myself and of human nature that I undertook, gave me the opportunity to have this look and see my culture with deeper eyes. It is said that sometimes we have to go on a long journey to come back to where we began and really know the place for the first time. T. S. Eliot puts it beautifully in his poem "Little Gidding":

> We shall not cease from exploration
> And the end of all our exploring
> Will be to arrive where we started
> And know the place for the first time.

My Spanish Mediterranean culture is characterized by qualities like vitality, *joie de vivre*, passion, sensuality, emotions, and artistry. They all show in how we live, our customs, our philosophy of living, our art, or our cuisine, and give the culture its characteristic aliveness and joy of living.

Millions of people from all over the world come every year to the Mediterranean for their vacations—not in vain; the Mediterranean is the top vacation destination in the world. They come not just for tourism purposes, but mostly to get renewed in body, heart, and soul by immersing themselves in the aliveness of this region and its cultures. When they leave, many say they wish they could bring a piece of the Mediterranean home with them, to keep them enjoying this aliveness and joy of living they experience while here.

Cultures have very specific ways of living and, as such, are not easy to translate from one part of the world to another, but principles are universal and, as such, independent of the specifics of a certain culture. Now that I am equipped with deeper psychological and spiritual insights, I can see the principles that underlie the vitality and joy of living of the Mediterranean cultures, but most importantly, I can see the principles that underlie humans' vibrant aliveness and, as a consequence, the Aliveness Factor principles of humans' joy of living, that joy of living that comes from our being and feeling vibrantly alive.

So drawing from the experiences of my personal journey, as well as my subsequent studies in humanistic psychology, and from my Mediterranean culture and life, I have come up with the following seven principles of vibrant aliveness.

1. A body filled with vitality and energy
2. Being present and in touch with the physical dimension of life
3. Flowing feelings
4. An open heart filled with love, joy, and passion
5. A deep connection with life
6. A fully expressed spirit
7. A soul imbued with enthusiasm, inspiration, and meaning

These seven principles have the power to bring vibrancy and aliveness to our being and joy of living to our lives. As you can see, most of them are self-explanatory, although others might seem less so. In part two, we will see all of them in more detail and within a practical framework that will present ways to activate them in anyone's life, independent of the culture where they live.

But before getting to there, I want to show you how many of these principles are ingrained, in one way or another, in the ways and customs of the Mediterranean cultures, bringing them their characteristic aliveness and joy of living.

The Mediterranean Way

I f there is something that has characterized the Mediterranean region over the centuries, it is the vitality and aliveness of its cultures. Having been the cradle of very rich civilizations, such as the Greeks, Egyptians, Romans, or Phoenicians, the Mediterranean has been an area of creativity, exchange, and dynamic interaction of cultures, which can account for the vitality inherent in the essence of its spirit. This, together with the warm temperature and abundant sun of the region that support the expansion and vibrancy of life, has created the vital cultures that inhabit this region, with Spain, my home country, being one of them.

Although each Mediterranean country may have its own idiosyncrasies, all the countries share common traits of character, lifestyle, and philosophy of living that are behind their characteristic vitality. In this chapter, I am going to do a quick review of them.

Let me begin with a question: Do you enjoy eating? I bet you do, because eating is one of the pleasures we human beings have. In my country, and in the Mediterranean countries in general, we have a rich cuisine that makes satisfying the need to feed ourselves an act of enjoyment. If we put together the different dishes that can be enjoyed in the various regions of the country, the list would be incredibly long. Over the centuries, there has been a creative impulse to convert the act of feeding oneself into an act of pleasure and enjoyment. Today, Spanish chefs are among the best in the world for their creativity and capacity to produce dishes that delight all the senses.

This shows the first trait that vitalizes the Mediterranean cultures: *a philosophy of enjoying life.* Enjoying life is in our cultural DNA, and food is its most obvious expression. We have produced, and keep producing, this rich cuisine just to enjoy it. The same can be said of our music, art, and design. All of them are imbued by the impulse to create and to enjoy the creation.

This attitude of enjoying life fills the Mediterranean cultures with vitality because it fills the hearts of people with joy—the fourth principle of a vibrant aliveness.

Of course, there are people in the Mediterranean countries who don't have this attitude toward life. The traits we are seeing are traits of the culture as a whole, and this doesn't mean that every single person enacts them. But being cultural traits, they are part of our collective spirit and customs, and hence present in the lives of a great majority.

Continuing with food, another characteristic of our cuisine is that it is based on what has come to be called "the Mediterranean diet."

One of the most important factors that affect our levels of physical vitality and energy is our diet—the nourishment we put into our bodies. Our diet needs to provide our bodies with all the energy and nutrients that they need to function, become renewed, and thrive, and any lack deprives us of vitality and can cause health problems.

In this regard, the diet structure upon which the different Mediterranean cuisines are based has been shown to be one of the best in the world. Although each Mediterranean country has its own cuisine, the primary components of all of the cuisines are the same, and this is what is called the Mediterranean diet.

Countless scientific studies have shown that it is this kind of diet that is behind the low levels of heart disease, obesity, diabetes, and cancer, as well as the high life expectancy that the residents of the Mediterranean countries enjoy. But beyond this fact, this diet also has enormous power to produce vitality. This is so because it is based mainly on fresh food and on components such as vegetables, fruits, legumes, or nuts that fill the body with their very alive life force. These, together with the healthy proteins that come from fish and the extremely healthy olive oil, create the perfect nutritional scheme to ground the health and vitality of the body—the first principle of a vibrant aliveness.

Also related to this first principle there is another vitality trait of the Mediterranean cultures: *outside life*. We love to be outside. In the villages, traditionally (and still today), people used to take chairs outside and sit with neighbors. When I was a child, we spent our summer vacations in the village where my mother was born. I loved this time very much not just because it was vacation time, but also because I was outside all day long with my brothers and cousins. But it was not only children who loved to be outside so much; adults loved it too. I remember that every afternoon, all our neighbors gathered outside to chat. This was so common that most of the houses had a built-in stone bench outside to facilitate this. Even today, when many of us live in towns and cities where it is more difficult to sit outside with neighbors, this custom is there and can be seen in our love for sitting in the terraces of bars and restaurants to gather with friends and enjoy being outside.

The fact is that the sun and natural light are important sources of physical vitality for human beings. Do you have the experience of going outside on a sunny day and feeling very good and alive? The sun is the source of life on planet Earth; without it life as we know it would be impossible. Plants and trees grow looking for it. It has always amazed me the nearly "impossible" shapes they may adopt in their search for the sun. This can be understood because the sunlight is for them a crucial source of nutrition that, through the process of photosynthesis, is transformed into the organic matter they need. In our case, we may not be photosynthetic creatures, but still we are nurtured and energized by the sunlight.

In the Mediterranean countries, we have the luck of having plenty of sun and plenty of sunny days—maybe this is the reason why we love to be outside so much. But sunlight is readily available throughout the world and ready to fill anyone with its energy, independent of where he or she lives (except maybe in the polar regions in the winter season). This is important to note because nowadays more and more people work in closed spaces illumined with artificial light and are getting little exposure to the natural light of the sun during their week. This prevents them from benefiting from this important source of vitality and overall well-being. Yes, this last one is an important and now provable point. In a recent study carried out in the United Kingdom with 1,250 people, the researchers found very important improvements in mood and self-esteem after just a few minutes of such outside activities as walking, gardening, cycling, fishing, boating, and horseback riding.

Another characteristic of the Mediterranean cultures is the *rootedness* we have with family and friends. This rootedness gives us a sense of connection and belonging—the fifth principle of a vibrant aliveness—that enlivens our hearts. It is quite normal for people to live all their lives in the city, village, or area where they were born and where their family lives. We love being with our people, with our family, and with our lifelong friends, and want to be close to them.

The family is the nuclear structure around which our lives are built. Even in today's times, when there is an increasing number of singles living alone, the extended family of parents, grandparents, brothers, sisters, aunts, uncles, nephews, nieces, and in-laws is still at the center of our lives, and we spend time with them on a very regular basis. The family is part of our identity, and although we are also experiencing the modern trend toward individualism, we still derive our sense of who we are in the bigger context of our family and lineage.

But our rootedness doesn't stop with the family; it also includes our ties with friends, and this shows in our social life. We love to socialize and to gather with friends; this is an important source of vitality and happiness for us. This fact is now backed by the researchers of the branch of psychology called Positive Psychology. They have produced significant evidence that shows that the happiest people are those with more active and richer social lives.

Sometimes when people from other countries learn that even on workdays, those of us in Spain take between one and two hours for lunch, they are a bit surprised, especially those from countries where lunch is a half-hour break for a quick snack. For us, lunch is not only a time to eat, but also a time to socialize and gather with others. This nourishes us as much as the food that we eat does, and fills us with vitality and energy for the second half of the day.

This last point shows another trait of the Mediterranean cultures: *life balance.* Music is possible because of the time between notes; written language is possible because of the space between letters; the same way, we human beings need time off work in order to have a life and to rest and recover.

Although Mediterranean countries are following the dynamics of modern life with its increase in workload and pressures, still we have ingrained in our cultures a balance between our professional and personal lives. This balance allows us time to spend with family and friends, to enjoy life, and to replenish our energy. The Spanish custom of taking between one and two hours for lunch is a perfect example of it. This custom allows us not only to feed ourselves, but also to enjoy our meal, to socialize, and to rest and recover.

This custom might seem to be against the all-powerful productivity mandate of today's world, but upon further consideration, this is not so much so. Multiple studies have proved how our productivity gets significantly reduced when we are fatigued or stressed. Productivity in today's modern knowledge work has lost its strong connection with the number of hours we work and has become more and more dependent on the capacity we bring to those hours. This fact has been very well-understood by some companies all over the world that are implementing work-life-balance policies, and creating rest and restoration areas on their premises for their employees.

These life-balance customs that are part of our culture are a source of aliveness for us because they are directly connected with three of the human aliveness principles. First of all, they help us to replenish our physical vitality and energy—the first principle. Secondly, they allow us time to enjoy life—the third principle. And thirdly, they facilitate our spending time with family and friends—the fifth principle.

All the traits that we have seen so far are a source of aliveness for us; however, all of them belong to the realm of cultural traits and customs, and this list wouldn't be complete if it didn't include other traits that are more related to character. In this regard, there are three character traits that stand out: physicality, expressiveness, and outgoing and light spirit.

Our physicality shows in our taste for the sensual world. We love to touch life with our senses, our hands, and our bodies. Although we experience, as other people in the developed world, the virtualization of life and the movement toward mind experience that the digital revolution has brought, we, as a culture, are still very connected with the physical dimension of life, and love physical experience.

When we go out into the sunshine, what we are having is a physical experience; we are feeling the sun on our skin and our bodies. When we enjoy a delightful meal, we are dueling in the realm of the senses, letting all the tinges of flavor and aroma touch us. When we talk to others, we communicate with our bodies as much as with our mouths. This physicality is a source of connection with the physical world and of pleasures and joy—the second principle.

On the other hand, that the Mediterranean people are very expressive can be noticed immediately at the sight of two or more having a conversation; they move and make gestures, they touch each other, they talk aloud, they are impulsive . . . . It is difficult for us to stand still. As a culture, we are emotional and expressive.

An artistic example of this emotionality and expressiveness can be found in the Spanish flamenco music and dance. When you see a flamenco performance, what you see is pure expression, emotion, and passion made into moving art. It doesn't necessarily have to express joy; it can express sorrow, but the aliveness of it is unquestionable.

Emotions and impulses are life energy that, when flowing and given expression, enliven us. They enliven our bodies, our hearts, and our spirits—the third and sixth principles. Although not all the Mediterranean people have the same degree of expressiveness or emotionality, which also depends on the individual character, the culture as a whole has this trait, and to one degree or another, we all live it out because it is the environment in which we grow up.

The third character trait that enlivens the Mediterranean peoples is our outgoing and light spirit, which tends to lean on the bright side of life. We take any opportunity to celebrate, get together, and have fun. We love to have fun and laugh. It is quite normal to see people in bars, in restaurants, and at social events laughing and having a great time together. This is a source of vitality for us because it fills our hearts with joy—the fourth principle. But this is also a source of health; fun and laughter have been proved to improve our physical and emotional health, as mind-body medicine has shown. They, for instance, improve the functioning of the immune system. Maybe this is another reason behind the higher longevity that the Mediterranean citizens enjoy.

I want to finalize this quick review of the cultural and character traits that vitalize the Mediterranean peoples with the one that somehow encompasses all of them: our *passion for life*. In general, the Mediterranean people are people who love life and living. Historically, the sparkling vitality that the different civilizations that have inhabited this area have shown can only be understood by this passion for life.

Although each one of us has our own personality, some being more passionate than others, some more emotional, and others more intellectual, the delight in living and passion for life is part of our collective spirit and permeates our way of being in life and living our lives.

As a summary, the cultural and character traits that vitalize and give joy of living to the Mediterranean cultures are the following:

- A philosophy of enjoying life
- Strong ties with family and friends
- An active social life
- Life balance
- The Mediterranean diet
- Outside life
- Physicality
- Expressiveness
- Fun and laughter
- A passion for life

These are specific traits of the Mediterranean cultures, but as we've seen, they enact the more universal principles that we saw in the previous chapter.

Through this quick review, I wanted to give you an example of the principles in action. But most importantly, I wanted to show you how the Aliveness Factor is a major factor in humans' joy of living. The idiosyncratic joy of living of the Mediterranean cultures is proof of it.

Does this mean that everybody in the Mediterranean is happy and vibrantly alive the way we've seen in the previous chapter? No. My own case proves it. We are human beings like any other people and face similar challenges and issues. What happens is that the Mediterranean cultures, as a whole, are vital and joyful cultures, and this helps in that human quest for happiness and joy of living.

PART II

A PRACTICAL METHOD FOR VIBRANT ALIVENESS

I have read quite a few self-help books in my life, and sometimes I have thought that they were very thoughtful treatises on the subject but lacked in practicality for readers to translate the insights into results in their own lives. This is why I decided from the very beginning that this book had to provide the reader, you, with practical and actionable information that will bring results.

The outcome is a framework of seven steps that will bring vibrancy to your body, heart, and soul, and joy of living to your life. Each step is associated with one of the aliveness principles we've seen in part one, and constitutes a major initiative you can take to activate that principle in your life. Because they are based on universal principles, these steps are culture-independent and designed to help any person, regardless of where he or she lives, get vibrantly alive and experience the joy of living that this brings.

Here are the seven steps:

- *Move your way into vitality.*
- *Get out of your mind and into your senses.*
- *Feel your feelings.*
- *Connect deeply with life.*

- *Rekindle your* joie de vivre.
- *Swim in your own river.*
- *Fill your life with enthusiasm, inspiration, and meaning.*

The steps are presented in a logical order that creates a powerful progression when you follow it step by step, but you don't need to follow this order if you don't feel drawn to do so; you can work with any of the steps separately.

I know from experience that personal development can be a long journey, as long as you want it to be. But it doesn't need to be a long process to get significant results and see changes in your life experience. Sometimes it only takes a simple change of attitude or a simple initiative, such as deciding to introduce in your life something that you love doing, to experience a significant change in your aliveness and joy of living.

The seven steps are a good framework that can help you. But I want to warn you: A system is that—a system; in itself, it doesn't produce any results. What produces results is action. In getting any result we want in life, a good strategy or system is very important, but the real key is action, actually doing something to get what we want or where we want to be.

If you have felt drawn to this book, I guess that you may be feeling a need or a desire for more aliveness and joy in your life. Maybe the title or maybe a word or a phrase you've read in the book has touched this longing in you. This is a very important clue because the nature of living organisms is that they feel attracted to that which they need the most. So you have arrived at where you need to be. My responsibility is to help you fulfill your need with all that I have. Your responsibility is to take action.

Therefore, I really encourage you to begin this second part of the book with this intention in mind. Your intention will pave the way to the actions that will fulfill your desire.

In the next seven chapters, we are going to see the seven steps to a vibrant and joyful life.

CHAPTER FOUR

Move Your Way
into Vitality

Our being and feeling vibrantly alive begins in our physical dimension, in our bodies. The more vital and vibrant our bodies are, the more vibrant and alive we are, and the more we experience the joy of being alive.

There are different aspects that affect our levels of physical vitality, but for the purposes of this seven-step process, I am going to focus on one that is key and that has the power to boost one's level of vitality significantly and in a very short time: physical activity.

There is a trend in our modern society that has been growing over the last decades and that now has reached the level of an epidemic in urban populations—the trend toward sedentary life. Studies show that as much as 80 percent of urban citizens are sedentary, meaning that individuals spend less than 10 percent of the day physically active (in which case they would deploy at least four times as much energy as when at rest).

This has consequences not only on our health, but also on our physical vitality. Our bodies are designed to be physically active. Actually, during 99 percent of our existence as a species, human beings have had very physically active lives. This is in our genes and body setup. Our bodies need physical activity to function well, and they thrive on it. If they don't have it, they get sick. On the contrary, when we move our bodies, our health improves, and our physical vitality increases.

One of the things I have seen again and again in both myself and others is the effect that moving our bodies has on our levels of physical and emotional vitality. Every time I do a workout at the gym, take a movement class, or just take a walk, I experience an activation in my body; the energy seems to get switched on and begin flowing, my mind gets clearer, and preoccupations tend to go away, being replaced by positive emotions.

However, nowadays we live in a society characterized by sedentary lifestyles. Our work has become more sedentary than ever, especially in cities, and we spend more and more of our leisure time sitting in front of our TVs and computers. We don't even need to move to go shopping if we don't want to! As comfortable and convenient as all this is, the price we are paying is a high one in terms of compromised health, decreased vitality, and a diminished sense of aliveness.

If you already have a physically active life, you may want to skip this step, but if not, I highly encourage you to begin your journey into aliveness here. Even if you are already physically active, reading this step may give you some new ideas and perspectives that can be helpful to enjoy your physical activity and your life more.

Beyond the benefit of increased vitality, the habit of physical exercise brings numerous health benefits:

- A reduction of arterial tension (also called the silent assassin—high blood pressure)
- Weight reduction and the prevention of obesity
- Less risk of developing diabetes
- The prevention of heart and cardiovascular accidents
- Stress and anxiety reduction
- A lessening of depression

It could be said that physical exercise is the cheapest drug on earth. It has a very positive effect not only on our physical health, but also on our psychological well-being. In a study conducted by the Mayo Clinic, researchers showed that physical activity has a very positive impact on reducing levels of stress, anxiety, and depression, psychological conditions that are affecting more and more people nowadays.

But if physical exercise is so good—and so necessary—for us, why isn't it part of everybody's life? Why is the sedentary trend rising so much? I think the answer can be found in the realms of education, habits, cultural trends, and misunderstandings.

It surprises me that adults become so sedentary because as children, we really love moving our bodies—running, chasing, jumping, ... It seems that as we age, we forget how much joy our bodies can bring.

When I was in school, once a week, we had a class called physical education, which was more about gymnastics and sports than education. Some weeks we spent the class in the gym practicing gymnastics, and other weeks we played sports, namely soccer or basketball. Although I welcomed this class because it was outside the classroom and the normal routine, I cannot say that I loved it. The gymnastics classes were more about passing an exam than about having fun enjoying being in our bodies and moving them. On the sports side, I didn't enjoy those two sports very much. The end result was that I didn't develop any enjoyment of physical activity and an understanding of how beneficial it is. The education system placed much more emphasis on performance and competition than on really educating us on the importance of exercise and on facilitating our enjoying and loving it. This is sad news, taking into account how beneficial and important physical activity and exercise are for our health and our aliveness. So, though most of us have an intellectual, and even an intuitive, understanding of the benefits of physical activity, in many cases, it wasn't part of our education. The consequence was that we didn't develop the habit and the love for it. Thus, we don't have the inner pull that can help to counteract the cultural trends of our time.

First of all, physical exercise does not have to be equated with gym workouts, running, or practicing sports; these are very good ways to do it, but not the only ones. It is important to make the distinction between exercise and physical activity. You can be physically active just by walking every day a certain amount of time, or gardening, or dancing, or practicing yoga, or playing games with your kids outside, or . . . you name it. The key is to get your body in action, spending at least four times as much energy as it does at rest.

So you have plenty of options to choose from to introduce physical activity to your lifestyle and get all the benefits of it. But bear in mind a very important factor: Choose something that you really enjoy, and have fun doing it. Enjoyment is important, since joy enlivens our hearts, but there is more to it: When you choose an activity that you enjoy, it will strengthen your motivation to do it, and the activity itself will be pulling you instead of you having to push and to make the effort to keep the practice.

In addition, the psycho-physical benefits of physical exercise will be higher when doing something you enjoy. Today's mind-body medicine research has shown us the effects of our state of mind on our physical health and well-being. For instance, Dr. Lawrence LeShan, considered one of the fathers of mind-body therapy, has helped certain cancer patients develop ways of being with themselves, with others, and with the world that lead to greater enthusiasm and satisfaction in their lives, and he has clearly shown that this enthusiasm and satisfaction has an amazing effect on their recovery.

So, fun and enjoyment are not only a pleasant experience, but also a factor in our health and well-being. If we find the physical activity that provides us with the exercise that so greatly benefits us and, in addition, enjoyment and fun, well, the end result can be extremely powerful.

I first became aware of this in that month I spent at Esalen Institute. After the morning movement classes, I always felt that I was vibrant with energy and life. It was like my whole being had been switched on and electricity flowed through me, giving me a sensation of vibrancy and aliveness that extended through my day. It was not only the physical activation itself, but also the joy and fun I had with it. These two had an effect on my emotions and uplifted my spirit. Physical activity was not strange for me; I was used to gym workouts and running, but in the movement classes, I found something I loved and enjoyed so much.

Once, in a course I was conducting with corporate executives, we were talking about the benefits of finding your activity, and one of the participants said, "My life changed when I began to play tennis." I was curious about such a strong statement and asked him to tell us a bit more about it. He said:

> Over the years, I had gradually lost much of the zest and motivation that I had at work when I began my career, so much so that this was taking a toll on my whole life.
>
> Then, a few years ago, together with some work colleagues, we decided to begin practicing tennis after work. We began taking classes and playing a couple of days a week, eventually moving into playing nearly every day.
>
> I loved it so much that it made my day. I would wake up every day with the enthusiasm for the match we were going to play in the afternoon, so much so that my day at the office would go smoother, my mood was more positive, and I had more fun doing my work; even the relationship with my wife got better because of this better mood I had. And all of it was because of the daily tennis match!
>
> Today, tennis has become a very important part of my life.

This was a double lesson for me and for all the other participants in the course: It is never too late to begin a sport or an activity—when this guy started playing tennis, he was well into his fifties—and when we find the physical activity that is right for us, the effects on our lives can be amazing.

So my question for you now is, What physical activities do you love? Any particular sport? Running in nature? Dancing? Swimming? Skating? Doing yoga? Participating in aerobics? Doing any particular mode of body movement? Biking? Trekking? What is it that you love?

If there is nothing in particular that comes to your mind, which physical activities did you love when you were a kid or a teenager, in high school, at the university?

When answering this question, don't let yourself down by thinking, *Well, I don't have the time for this; it will be difficult; I am an adult now* . . . . All this thinking comes from an aspect of our psyches that we could call the saboteur, which tends to sabotage our own well-being and happiness.

Bear in mind that our bodies need and want physical activity, that when we are children and function on natural impulses, we tend to get physically active and enjoy it. But we may have developed a habit that overshadows this natural way of our biology and makes us feel less inclined to get into physical activity. In our lives, we have developed habits. Some of them are good, such as brushing our teeth to keep them healthy, but others are not—for instance, smoking or overeating—even though they exert a pull on us. The breaking of habits is always a bit of a challenge, but it is perfectly possible if we use the right strategies. When you find an activity that you love, this love will pull you and help you to develop the habit of engaging in it regularly.

I know that today, it is a challenge for many of us to get time to engage in a certain "leisure" activity; work and family responsibilities sometimes don't leave much room for it. But I have found that in these cases, the challenge is to get creative and to make some adjustments in your life to create this space. Even in very tight schedules, we can normally find a way to fit in a physical activity that brings us enjoyment and fun at least once or twice a week. Then we can complement this activity with the most basic, yet powerful, of all physical activities: walking.

Walking is the most basic of all the physical activities, but is very effective. Between half an hour and an hour of walking every day can bring enormous benefits to your health and vitality. And the good news is that together with being the most basic, it is also the most flexible. You can park your car at a certain walking distance from your work, you can get off the bus one bus stop before yours, or you can just go for a walk before or after work. The only requirement is that you walk at a fast pace so that your cardiovascular system gets pushed beyond its normal resting state. If you walk in nature, that's much better.

Get creative, though; you can do different things every day. The key factor is to realize how important physical activity is for you, your health, your aliveness, and your joy of living, and to take action.

If you introduce in your life the regular practice of a physical activity that you love—that brings you joy and fun—and complement it with some other physical activity on a daily basis, you will be taking a major step ahead in the objective of being and feeling vibrantly alive.

Together with exercise, a good diet and restoration time are also important components of our vitality. It is necessary that you recover the energy you spend. The two ways for this are through the time you give yourself for rest and recovery, and through what you eat. With respect to the first, statistics show that modern society is more and more sleep-deprived, with an increasing number of people sleeping on a daily basis between one and one and a half hours less than we need, which is around seven to eight hours a day. In addition, modern information technology, especially smartphones, has us "hooked" all the time, preventing us from disconnecting in search of recovery and restoration. So, seek ways to disconnect and recover during the day and to give yourself the sleep that as a living organism you need.

With respect to the diet, it is important that it is well-balanced and vitality-producing. In this regard, as we have seen, the Mediterranean diet is outstanding. As part of the additional resources for this book, you have a chart with the structure of this diet and some more information about it that you can use as a guide for healthy, vital eating. In the Resources section at the end of the book, you will find how to get it.

Following this first step will fill your body with vitality and vibrancy, creating the perfect ground for your vibrant aliveness.

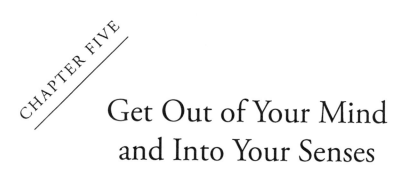

Get Out of Your Mind and Into Your Senses

In step one, we have focused on our body and on getting it vital and vibrant. In this second step, we are going to move into the realm of our consciousness and how it affects our aliveness.

In the same way that conditions of modern life are steering more and more people to a sedentary lifestyle, those same conditions are taking more and more people to increasingly live "in their heads."

Nowadays, an increasing number of people (65 to 70 percent in developed countries) are what has been termed "knowledge workers," meaning that they work applying knowledge and processing and manipulating information, with computers and digital devices as the main tools. This is a very important shift, from physical work to mental work, that has taken place in the last few decades.

In addition, leisure time is spent more and more in front of screens: the TV, the cinema, the computer, and videogames, which take us to virtual/mental experiences and away from experiencing the real, physical world.

All this has created a rich mental life that is wonderful because it has enriched our life experience. However, there is a flip side to this as well: the increasing disconnection from the body, from the senses, and overall from the physical dimension of life.

Have you ever driven to someplace, only to realize that you don't remember the places you've gone through because you were in your mind, thinking through things?

Have you ever finished your lunch, only to realize that you didn't even taste your food because you were in your thoughts?

Have you ever gone to a park and after breathing deeply realized how good it feels to feel "in touch" with nature and with your body, and how much more alive you feel?

A consequence of this moving into the mind's realm is a diminished aliveness because literally our life force is dialed down, and also because we lose connection with a primary and vibrant dimension of life: the physical dimension. Another consequence has to do with our enjoyment of life: we lose part of our capacity to enjoy all the pleasures and delights of the physical world.

This is a major imbalance of modern life that needs to be corrected. It is not that we have to stop using our minds, knowledge, and intelligence, or that we have to leave our work or stop going to the cinema or watching our favorite TV show. No, it is all about rebalancing and regaining equilibrium between our mental life and our direct experience of life.

One of the most important things I discovered in my journey was the state of mind called "presence." This is the state of mind that all spiritual and wisdom traditions talk about and that modern psychology has adopted. This is a state of awareness without thought. If you have ever experienced any kind of meditation, you know what I am talking about. If not, I invite you to do either of the following two experiments in order to bring the term from concept to experience. (I offer you two possibilities because you might find one easier than the other.)

Experiment I

Close your eyes, and take a few deep breaths to settle you and put you in a state of calm. Then put your hand on your belly and breathe normally. Put your attention on sensing, as you breathe, the movement of your belly where you have put your hand. After a minute or so, expand your attention to the whole process of the breathing. It may happen that your attention goes to your head and you move to thinking. This is not a problem; it is normal; just, when you realize it, move your attention back to your belly and breathing.

In a very short time, you will be in a state of attention without thought. You will be in a state of presence; you will be "in touch."

Experiment II

With your eyes open, select something from your environment— an object, the door, the wall, a plant, a tree, the sky, the clouds, the horizon—then close your eyes and take a few deep breaths to settle you and put you in a state of calm. When you feel calm, open your eyes, and put your attention on whatever you have chosen. You can look at the shape, the color, or some detail in it, but don't get into thinking. It is normal that the object brings thoughts and images to you or that you may begin thinking about some of its details. If this happens, become aware that you have moved into the mind, and come back to the experience of just contemplating that thing, of just having a purely visual experience. When this happens, you are in direct "touch" with that thing; you are in direct experience versus mental experience. You are present.

The state of presence is a state of pure awareness. It is not thinking; it is not imagining; it is not reflecting; it is not concepts; it is not ideas; all of these belong to the realm of our mind. Presence is awareness and contact.

If you have chosen the clouds in the sky as the object of your contemplation, you are in the state of presence when you are just observing them, their shapes, their colors, how they move. On the contrary, being in the mind would mean reflecting on what you are seeing: "This is so beautiful. Look at that little cloud; it looks like a baby bear. Well, it seems that it's going to rain; it's getting too dark; I'd better take my coat to my appointment this afternoon. By the way, I should have told Jean to go buy some more bread for tonight's dinner," and on, and on, and on. The deeper we get into our internal dialogue and reasoning and planning and remembering, the more we lose touch with the real experience.

The principle of awareness is the most basic aspect of our being, so much so that all the spiritual traditions have termed it "the ground of being." Why call it so?

Think about this: None of the cells of our bodies are more than seven years old. Our body is constantly dying and being reborn; cells are dying and birthing all the time. Within our minds, something similar happens. Its contents also keep changing (in neuroscience, this is called the doing and undoing of synapses between neurons). Even memories of the past don't remain the same over time. So, who are we? What is it that gives us the sense of permanent identity, of continuity? It is our consciousness, our capacity for being aware. This is why this aspect of our being is called the ground of being.

Our thoughts come and go; our emotions come and go; our bodies are a process of life in permanent flow and change, but we are the witness, the consciousness that can be aware of all of it. This consciousness is our ultimate essence and the life force that animates us. When we are present, we are strongly connected with this life force; this is why our being present enlivens us. On the contrary, when we "live in our heads," our life force is dialed down and so to our aliveness.

The state of presence is very gratifying because it gives us a sense of being grounded and alive, but also because it heightens our experience. This is so because we are in touch. It is not the same to look at a tree with the mind, through the filter of all the information we have in our minds about trees, as through the state of presence, in which we can "experience" the actual tree we are looking at.

On one occasion, I took a group outside after a whole day of an indoor training course. The idea was to go to nature just to relax, have some fun, and disconnect in order to recharge batteries for the next day. I had prepared a few games to make this time outside richer and more fun; one of them was a sensory perception experiment. I divided the group in pairs and gave them a piece of cloth they could use to wrap around the eyes of one of them. The idea was that the person with the wrapped eyes had to experience with all the senses except sight—hearing, taste, smell, and touch, while the other person looked after her. I decided to cancel the sight sense because it is very strong in our attention, and this made it easier to bring awareness to the other senses. I gave them instructions to leave their "heads" and come into their senses; then they began to wander around in an area full of trees, bushes, plants, stones, soil . . . . I immediately noticed something: Even though I had told them to stay in their sensory experience, the person with the wrapped eyes tended to get into verbal definition and begin to tell his partner about the characteristics of what he was exploring: It feels like . . ., it smells like . . ., it tastes like . . . . We are so used to living in our minds that we tend to disconnect from real experience and come into the information we have stored in our heads. Also, we are so used to words, we find it difficult to stop talking (either externally or internally), to silence our minds and just listen, perceive, and experience.

The state of presence connects us with the real experience that is happening here and now. When we are in our minds, we are in the realm of concepts and abstraction, but also we tend to be away from the now, dwelling either in the future or the past. This last point is another reason why the state of presence feels so good, because it not only connects us with life, but also gives us a break from all the anxiety-producing workings of our minds that come from worries about the future and ruminations and regrets about the past.

Our mind is a tremendous gift and capacity of our human nature. We must be aware, however, of how we use it and where we are centered. We can use our mind and all the power it has, we can learn and use that knowledge, we can enjoy the world of concepts, ideas, information, the cinema, the Internet, videogames . . . and still live very much centered in the ground of our being, in our presence.

Although mental experiences can be fun and rewarding, the physical world is a source of numerous pleasures that we can enjoy— food, music and sounds, smells, touch, beauty—and the more present we are, the more we can enjoy it all. Likewise, the experience of our bodies is a source of pleasures, feelings and sensations being the source. The more into our bodies we get, the more physical we get, the more we can enjoy our bodies and being in the body. For instance, our sexual experiences, something that normally connects us with basic life, are greatly enhanced when we are truly in the body and can experience its sensations and feelings.

Also, our being present in our body and connected with sensations and feelings makes our body more vibrant and alive because the life force is directly channeled to it, much like when we plug in a water boiler, it brings the energy of the water, its temperature, up.

In order to be more present in our lives, and reap all its benefits and rewards, we can practice the state of presence. As with any other thing that we can develop, practice is what gets us to where we want to be.

In this regard, one of the best practices that can be adopted is meditation. Even though meditation is a practice that is rooted in the spiritual traditions of the world, nowadays, it has become mainstream for its many benefits to our health and well-being. Today, there are thousands of studies that back the benefits of getting into a peaceful state of pure awareness.

I really encourage you to give meditation a try if you have never tried it. There are different kinds of meditation, and you can always find the one that suits you best. As part of the additional resources for this book, I have recorded a simple meditation exercise that can give you a taste of it. In the Resources section, you will find a way to get it.

However, although we can count by the millions the number of people who nowadays practice some kind of meditation on a regular basis, I have found that for many people, it is not easy to sit down, close one's eyes, and get into a meditative state. Also, it can be a difficult practice to maintain for people with hectic and very busy lives. This is why I want to present to you another practice that is very effective and also a delight. I call it "presencing."

This practice is about introducing into your life moments when you consciously get into a state of presence; you get out of your head, your thinking, your planning, your processing information, your talking (either external or internal talk), and come into inner silence, into listening mode, into your senses. These are moments to taste life, to taste the physical world, to feel yourself.

We get into presencing by bringing our attention to the experience of the present moment, and more precisely to:

- What comes from our senses: what we see, hear, smell, taste, sense
- The sensations of our bodies
- How we feel—any feelings or emotions that we are currently experiencing

When we bring our attention to our senses, they become heightened, and our experience is heightened as well. But the most important thing is that we can taste and enjoy the physical world the same way we do when we enjoy the delicate flavors of exquisite food or wine.

By connecting with our bodies and our feelings, our bodies also get more vibrant—our very presence enlivens the body—and we can feel this aliveness and enjoy it. Just imagine how alive your body is with all its cells, organs, and metabolism functioning all the time, but better than this, don't imagine it; pause for a minute, and feel it because life is something to be experienced, not just thought about.

By presencing ourselves and the outside world, we have the opportunity to taste and enjoy the flavors and vibrancy of life. The more we do it consciously, the more this awareness gets integrated into our consciousness and the more alive we will be and feel.

Unlike meditation, where you need to set some time apart and withdraw attention from the outside and move it to the inside, you can practice presencing on many occasions throughout the day. It is very flexible. You can become present while:

- You walk to work
- Having a relaxed moment sitting in your garden
- On a walk in a park
- Sitting on a terrace, watching people walk by
- Having lunch or dinner
- Enjoying a cup of coffee
- Having a break at work when you just sit back and observe your environment
- Contemplating the beauty of natural scenery or a sunset
- Contemplating your kids playing in the park
- Doing almost anything

All it takes is the intention to get "in touch" for a moment and to savor life. How long? It can be for just a minute, but I am sure that when you get used to these moments of inner calm and connection, you will naturally want to have them for longer.

Practice getting into presencing mode several times a day. Take every opportunity that you have to leave your mind for a little while and get into the ground of your being. Give yourself the present of the delight of it. Look at the word I just used, "present"; the state of presence, to be present, is really a gift—a present we can give ourselves.

If possible, go outside, and get into presencing mode—take a walk, sit on a park bench, allow yourself to be bathed by the sunlight while you are fully present.

If you already practice some kind of meditation, still I really encourage you to introduce in your life the practice of presencing because of how powerful it is as a complement to your meditation and to help you introduce in your day moments of reconnection.

On the other hand, if you don't practice meditation, I encourage you to try it and if you like it to incorporate its practice into your life on a daily basis. Meditation has so many positive effects that the investment of just fifteen minutes will come back to you exponentially.

Consciously practicing presencing is a way to enjoy life. Spending time presencing is a way to enjoy and to experience more of life and of ourselves, but also to calm our minds, to reduce our stress, and to bring serenity and joy into our lives.

These can become moments of real pleasure and enjoyment, moments to savor the experience of being alive and to bask in the serenity that lies at the very center of your being.

CHAPTER SIX

Feel Your Feelings

Once, when I was attending a one-week residential workshop, something happened that touched me deeply. Well into the week, the facilitators had managed to create a close and intimate atmosphere in the group. It must have been the third or the fourth day when a man in his mid-thirties began to cry uncontrollably. He couldn't stop; it was like the doors of a dam had burst open, and the water was being released. We all were deeply touched to witness this big guy, who seemed so controlled and intelligent in his comments and remarks, just break open suddenly and fall into the waters of feeling and emotion. This situation continued for the following two days. By the end of the week, his emotions had tempered, and he was obviously feeling great. His face was shining, and he looked so much more alive.

When we are cut off from our feelings, we experience a sort of numbness that we might not even be aware of until we have an experience like this man had. In his case, it was clear that he was a very controlled and mind-centered man with pent-up emotions. Once he was in an inviting and safe environment, those emotions found release. When he got in touch with his feelings and let them flow, he felt enlivened, even if what he was experiencing were feelings of sadness and grief. I believe that most of that grief came precisely from his being cut off from his feelings, maybe for most of his life. After his sadness and grief got released, his heart was cleansed, open, and able to experience emotions like joy and love that made his heart vibrantly alive.

When we are in touch with our feelings and let them flow, our hearts, our emotional dimension, are more alive, and so are we. This doesn't mean we have to give expression to all our feelings and let them control us or get us into difficult situations. It means that we don't deny our feelings, that we acknowledge them, feel them, and let them be. In order for us to have vibrant hearts filled with love, joy, and passion, we need to be in touch with our hearts and our feelings, and allow any difficult emotions that might live in us be healed and cleansed.

As we've seen in the previous chapter, the ways of our modern life lead us to dwell more and more in the realm of the mind, bringing with it the side effect of our feelings losing presence in our consciousness, but there are also other reasons why we may have our feeling capacity lessened.

It may have happened that we grew up in a family environment that was not supportive of our feelings. Maybe the open expression of feelings was not okay, and we had to neglect our feelings in order to be accepted. This practice became habit and eventually led us to disconnecting from those feelings.

Cultural conditioning is another factor that can get in the way of our feelings. There is, for instance, a cultural myth that says that feelings and emotions are women's issues. If a man displays any kind of emotional life, it can be seen as weakness or not being masculine. This is a pity because keeping emotions pent-up can prevent men from experiencing the emotional realm of their being and the joy, love, and passion that make our hearts vibrantly alive. This can have negative consequences, too, because pent-up emotions and feelings can cause havoc in our lives, make us sick, and create all sorts of problems in our relationships.

In addition, there is another potent reason behind the diminished-feeling life of many people: their own life experiences. Throughout our lives, we may go through experiences that mean pain for us, be it physical or emotional, and that leads us to numb ourselves in order to cope. Pain can be so overwhelming, especially for the most sensitive people, that we react by contracting our muscles and disconnecting from feeling. In a sense, we can say that we freeze, and we can remain there for years and years, even for a lifetime. If this is our case, we need to treat our disconnection with love and respect because it helped us to cope and protected the precious gift that our heart is.

If you resonate with the numbing of feeling that I have been talking about, then it is important that you do something to reawaken your feeling experience. This will advance your aliveness and your capacity to experience joy, love, and passion in your life.

By doing the presencing practice that I described in the previous chapter, you will be taking a step toward connecting with your own flow of feelings. By connecting with your body and becoming aware of it, you are facilitating the experiencing of your feelings and emotions because they happen in your body; we feel our feelings and emotions in our bodies.

In addition, there is a powerful and simple practice that helps a great deal to enhance our feeling experience: *conscious breathing*.

Breathing is the most important of all our bodily functions; without breathing, we die, and not breathing is a sure symptom of being dead. All the various yoga and bodywork modalities as well as certain therapies put especial emphasis on breathing because of its power to vitalize and loosen up the body.

When we breathe deeply, a high quantity of oxygen is brought to our cells. This results in a stronger production of vital energy. Likewise, deep and slow breathing loosens up our muscles, allowing us to experience much more vividly our feelings and emotions. When our muscles are tight, it is difficult to feel anything; actually, the tightening of our muscles is something we do to prevent feeling pain. Try something now; tense as much as possible all your body—tense and tighten your muscles as much as you can. What do you feel? For sure, you will feel the tension, but this will be all you can feel because such tightened musculature can't vibrate and channel the more subtle energies of the heart.

So the more we loosen our muscles, the more we will be able to feel. This doesn't mean that our muscles are not strong or don't have tone; it means they are not tense or tight (either on their surface layers or in the most inner structures).

Likewise, by putting our attention on our bodies with the intention of loosening our muscles and to enhance our capacity to feel, we are both helping the opening up of the feeling channel and actually facilitating being able to experience those feelings.

Deep breathing and conscious awareness are powerful tools for enhancing our emotional aliveness and our feeling alive. So breathe deeply, and consciously experience the aliveness of your body and the feelings of your heart.

In fact, I propose you stop reading now and spend the next five minutes doing the following breathing exercise.

Put the book aside, and if you are not sitting, take a seat, and let your body get loose and relaxed; feel all your weight falling into the seat.

Begin breathing, paying attention to filling up your lungs around 50 percent more than you usually do; just go this far beyond your normal breath but without forcing the full fill-up of the lungs. When exhaling, just let go of the air without forcing it out. Let the breathing be as free as possible—don't control it; just pay attention to filling your lungs more than usual but without doing controlled breathing.

Once you are settled on this rhythm, bring your attention to how you feel. Don't force anything. Just feel your body and the emotional state you have at the moment; maybe you can identify a feeling of excitement for something that you are going to do today, or maybe a feeling of sadness bubbles up. It also might happen that you cannot identify any emotional state. Don't worry if this is the case—just pay attention to the sensations of the air coming in and out of your body.

Stay there for a little while, letting yourself be in the experience. It is more than probable that your attention will move from feeling to mind; when this happens, don't get caught into the stream of thought. The moment you realize it, bring your attention back to feeling.

After five minutes or so, gently allow your attention to return to your reading.

It might happen that you connect with certain unpleasant emotions, such as sadness or grief or rage, that you don't want to feel. Well, this is what happens when we feel: We feel everything. The partial comfort of dimming our feeling of certain undesired feelings and emotions comes with the price of dimming the positive ones, too. Notice that I have used the term "partial comfort" because even if we don't consciously feel them, they are still in us, and even living below the conscious line, they are affecting us. It is a better strategy to acknowledge your deep feelings and then work with them. If, for instance, you notice a deep feeling of sadness, you can allow yourself to connect with it to learn what it is about, what is behind it, and listen to your inner wisdom to reveal the answer. This requires the willingness to stand the uncomfortable feeling, but it is a much better strategy in the long run because by suppressing the uncomfortable feelings from your consciousness, you don't get rid of them; they just get pushed underneath the line of consciousness.

Instead, by letting the feeling reveal its reason for being, you will be able to fix the cause. It might happen that there is a deep need in your heart for more intimacy or for expressing who you are more fully, and your lack of attention to this need is producing that feeling of sadness. Bear in mind that discomfort is designed to inform us that there is something that needs our attention. If you feel some kind of pain in your body, it informs you that there is something that is not okay that you need to pay attention to and do something about. The same happens with emotions.

It is important to say that sometimes behind our numbing of feeling, there may be painful traumas and experiences that need to be addressed carefully. In these cases, the help of a good therapist is very advisable in order to have the support and technique that will facilitate the release of the pent-up pain and the healing of the trauma, freeing yourself from the past and opening the possibility of a fuller and richer experience of life. But in many cases, it is more a matter of family and cultural conditioning that can be undone with some conscious work on our own.

You can practice conscious breathing anytime throughout the day. Ideally, take several brief moments during the day to consciously breathe and pay attention to how you feel. By doing this, you reconnect with yourself, and you check how you are, emotionally speaking. This will create a sense of intimacy and connection with yourself that will be very reassuring, nurturing, and satisfying, besides giving the experience of heightened aliveness.

When you practice conscious breathing, you are also practicing the presencing of yourself, but using a special breathing technique to open up the flow of feeling.

The opportunities are endless. Just a couple of minutes suffice to connect with yourself and bring into your consciousness your feeling experience, and this can be done while you:

- Are in your car at a red traffic light.
- Are in the supermarket cashier line.
- Are on break at work while you have a cup of coffee.
- Are at home while you wait for the microwave to heat up your dinner.
- Walk to your car.
- Take a walk in the park.

The more you do it, the brighter your feelings and the bigger your capacity to experience a wider range of feelings. This will bring to you a richer life experience and a higher sense of being alive.

Besides the practice of conscious breathing, yoga and bodywork can be very helpful in opening up our bodies and the flow of feeling.

Although rooted in the Eastern traditions, the practice of yoga has become very widespread in the West for its many benefits to our physical and psychological health and well-being. There are many modalities, whose focus and way of practice vary. You may like and enjoy one kind and not others; they can be quite different. It all depends on your personality, needs, and body structure. This makes it advisable to try two or three kinds of yoga if you feel attracted to this practice so that you find the one that suits you best. The regular practice of yoga will keep your body invigorated and flexible, and hence more able to channel your feelings to your consciousness. This can be a very good physical activity too.

Regarding bodywork techniques, the most popular are the different kinds of massage, but there are many other modalities: Alexander technique, bioenergetics, Feldenkrais, core energetics, craniosacral, Watsu, and shiatsu, for example. All of them are more in the therapeutic field than massage, but for that reason, they can be very helpful in addressing the blockages that prevent us from the free flow of energy and emotion in our bodies.

As part of the additional resources I have prepared for the book, there is a little report on the different modalities of yoga and bodywork. In the Resources section at the back of the book, you will find how to get it.

CHAPTER SEVEN

Connect Deeply
with Life

I n this fourth step, we are moving into the wider realm of life. In steps one through three, we have focused on aliveness principles that were circumscribed to ourselves; in this one, however, we will see how and why the kind of relationship we have with life has an impact on our aliveness and joy of living.

Facebook has astounded all of us by the speed at which it has spread all over the world, reaching nearly 1 billion users within just a few years of its launch. Other Internet-based social media platforms also are booming. The eagerness and enthusiasm of the general public in embracing social media clearly demonstrates that connection is one of the most basic human needs. What these technologies do is simply that—they help people to be in touch with other people. We love this. We humans are social beings, and socializing is a source of joy in our lives.

But even though the number of users of social media platforms is growing so strongly, feelings of isolation and loneliness are on the rise, especially in big cities. I recently had a conversation with the director of an important holistic education center in New York City, and he told me, "In New York, loneliness is reaching the levels of an epidemic." It seems ironic that in such a thriving city, so many people experience the suffering and the dissatisfaction of feeling lonely. It is ironic that in the midst of all the communication technology we have developed and that helps us connect with others, so many people feel an unsatisfied need for connection.

The answer to this irony must lie somewhere else, and it has to do with the word "connection." We human beings have a need for connection with other human beings and, in more general terms, for connection with life. This connection goes beyond social interaction and the surface of life, and dives deep into the heart. It is in our hearts that we feel the need for connection, and it is in our hearts that we can find the satisfaction of this need.

What is happening today is that the dynamics of modern life tend to produce a shallower relationship with life, preventing the deeper connection that we need and long for in our hearts and, as a result, depriving people of aliveness and joy of living.

The same way a racehorse needs to gallop because its very nature is set up for that and the horse thrives on galloping, our human hearts need connection because the heart's very nature is set up for that. If we don't feel connected with life, we experience an underlying feeling of alienation, of separateness that causes dissatisfaction and certain suffering. On the contrary, when we feel connected with life, like the racehorse that gallops, our heart thrives and shines with vibrancy and aliveness—and so do we.

So, here lies another key to our being vibrantly alive—and to our experiencing joy of living: a deep, heartfelt connection with life. To achieve this, there are four realms, or dimensions, of life with which we can deeply connect: others, nature, the transcendent, and ourselves.

Indigenous tribes, for instance, had a connection with nature that has been very much lost in our modern life, especially in cities. They saw nature as something alive, as an expression of the life force that underlies all life, of which they were part. They saw themselves being part of a wider web of life and in connection with it. This connected them with life and enlivened their hearts.

On the contrary, our modern culture sees nature as resources to be exploited in order to create wealth. The irony is that by seeing it this way, we, as a civilization, are not only polluting and exhausting the planet to our present point of unsustainability; we also have alienated ourselves from the web of life and the life force that nature represents like nothing else.

Indigenous tribes all over the world refer to nature as Mother Nature, mother earth, or Pachamama, and have a relationship with it from a heart of belonging and gratitude that enlivens them and makes them feel connected. Is this naive in our era of science and technology? Not at all. The truth is that nature is very alive and that all life forms a web of life that is interconnected, with us being a part of it. Remember when you have gone on a hike to the mountains, or have sat by a river or a lake, surrounded by nature, or on the cliffs overlooking the ocean. How did you feel? What did you experience? I am sure you experienced different sensations and feelings, but one of them certainly must have been that you felt enlivened. This is so because nature literally vibrates with life in its purest sense; it is a beautiful dance of life that reconnects us with the life force that pulsates in everything, us included. Our very bodies are nature itself.

Another characteristic of modernity is the loss of transcendence. Modern thought is saturated with the scientific worldview, which if characterized by anything is its focus on the physical plane of reality and the negation of what can't be measured. This has left many people orphans of the sacred, living in a pure physical world made of dead matter. This, in a sense, numbs us because it deprives us not only of a dimension of our being, but also of a source of heart connection.

It is not a matter of practicing any kind of religion with a specific credo or set of beliefs; many of us in this era of science and reason just can't accept credos or beliefs for their own sake. I don't want to say that faith is useless or unimportant; I just want to point out that for many people, the loss of transcendence has come as a result of a view of life through the eyes of reason and science that, as of today, has not proved the existence of a transcendent dimension of life. But still, we human beings crave meaning and transcendence; deep in our hearts, we can feel this need. Is this craving a neurotic need, as some psychiatrists put it, or a natural thirst? Well, let me answer this question with other questions: Would we have thirst for water if there weren't any water? Would birds have wings if there were no wind? These are important questions to ponder because they point to what all spiritual traditions have been telling us: There is something more to life than what we can see with our eyes. May it be that our hearts, with their need for connection with the transcendent, are informing us of a dimension of life that is real, though belonging to a different dimension than the physical plane?

The reality is that as science goes deeper and deeper into our physical reality, it is getting closer and closer to the views of the ancient traditions that stated the existence of a transcendent dimension of life that is the source of all existence. Albert Einstein, one of the greatest scientists of the twentieth century, puts it beautifully:

> Everyone who is seriously involved in the pursuit of science becomes convinced that a spirit is manifest in the laws of the universe—a spirit vastly superior to that of man, and one in the face of which we with our modest powers must feel humble.

Connection with this transcendent spirit is a longing of our hearts and a way for them to feel connected and enlivened.

There is yet another important source of connection: ourselves. Together with the loss of transcendence, another side effect of modernity is the loss of depth in our lives. Many of us live simply by going through the motions, so to speak, dealing with our daily activities and responsibilities and not having time to reflect on our own lives. The result is that many people nowadays feel a sort of estrangement from themselves, a lack of depth and meaning in their lives. It is not surprising that depression is so much on the rise in our modern world, since one of its causes is the loss of meaning.

A heartfelt connection with these four realms—others, nature, the transcendent, and ourselves—connects us deeply with life, satisfying this need of our hearts and making them vibrant and joyful.

And now that we've reviewed these key connections, how do we go about improving them? Let's see some ideas about how to do just that.

Others

The best way to deepen our connection with others is to care for them, their well-being, their happiness, their fulfillment, their joy. When we care about other people having all these things that we want, and we relate to them with the intention of having a positive impact on these aspects of their lives, our hearts open and connect. The irony is that our intention to bring good to the other person will bring even greater good to us in the form of aliveness, meaning, and satisfaction.

We can begin with our own families if we feel there is room there for deeper caring and connection. Our friends and coworkers are the next natural realms to move to, and from there, we can move to a general attitude toward others that focuses on bringing good, whatever form it takes, to their lives in any interaction we have with them.

The deepest connection we can have with other human beings is intimacy. In intimate relationships, not necessarily sexual relationships, we open our hearts to the other person to show our deepest concerns, joys, and challenges. This experience is extremely nurturing for the heart because of the deep connection it feels with another human being and the support in its struggles. It is very important to have at least one or two people in our lives with whom we can have this level of connection—a spouse, best friends, and some family members are the natural candidates, but also, mentors, coaches, and therapists can be very good options for intimate relationships.

A special note: I also want to include in this "Others" section animals and pets because for many people, they are a source of company, caring, and love, and hence a source of heartfelt connection. The National Institute of Mental Health in the United States recognizes pet therapy as a type of psychotherapy for treating depression and other mood disorders. The institute affirms, "Being around pets appears to feed the soul, promoting a sense of emotional connectedness and overall well-being." Again, connection seems to be the key.

Nature

To deepen our connection with nature, it is important that we often go and spend time in it, ideally in wilderness areas or open spaces where there are not many people around, but if you live in a city, parks can be good, too.

To connect with nature, we need to let ourselves be fully immersed in its energy. I find that while practicing sports in a natural setting is a good way to be in nature, we tend to focus on the practice of the sport or on the competition, and this prevents us from going deep into the connection with the natural environment itself.

Walks and time spent sitting in silence are wonderful ways to strengthen our connection with the pulsating life of nature because they allow us to attune to its vibration, lowering the busyness of our minds and attuning to our inner natural rhythms.

Immersing oneself in a natural setting is like having a nurturing and relaxing bath. This is an image that I love when I go to nature: I let my whole being be bathed by the pulsating, vibrant, and fresh energy of Mother Nature.

We must, however, set our intention to connect with nature and quiet the mind to let this connection happen. Once in this relaxed state, just looking at the natural setting with wonder and gratitude for the support it provides us will open our hearts to connect; as we appreciate the trees, which clean the air for us by absorbing the carbon dioxide and releasing the oxygen we breathe, we acknowledge that we could not exist as we do if there were no trees!

Another good way to connect with nature is by gardening. By taking care of our garden with the intention of immersing ourselves in its energy and feeling the life that pulsates in all those plants and flowers, we will be connecting with nature on a deep level.

The Transcendent

The transcendent takes different shapes and meanings, depending on the tradition on which we have been raised. In the Christian tradition, which is the predominant in the Western world, it takes the form of God. In the East, for instance, in the Taoist tradition, it takes the form of the deep current and intelligence of life people call the Tao. In modern spirituality, the terms used are "spirit" and "higher consciousness."

The concept and the imagery we associate with the transcendent are not what matters because they can vary widely; it is important that we use the ones that are more familiar to us and with which we feel more comfortable. The key is the sense of the transcendent, of the sacred, that this concept gives us and with which we can connect.

A marvelous way to open up our hearts and connect them with the transcendent is by looking at life with a sense of wonder for the mystery it is and a sense of reverence for the depths from whence the universe arises.

Even though we are extremely intelligent and have created amazing technology—for example, the computer I am using to write this book—this technology pales in comparison to the complexity of our own brains. Can it be that our brains are a product of random interactions of dead particles of matter, or is there a creative principle, an intelligence, that is behind it? This is a good question to ponder because as science advances, the bigger the island of our knowledge, the larger the shoreline of the mystery. If we cannot believe that a god or transcendent spirit is at the depths of all that exists, we can always look at life with eyes of wonder for the mystery it is.

Wonder, reverence, and gratitude are inner qualities that will open up our hearts for connection with the transcendent.

Ourselves

To deepen the connection with ourselves, we need to spend time in the company of ourselves. The same way that intimacy with another person deepens the connection with him or her, intimacy with ourselves deepens our own inner connection.

We live in a time when we have so many things to do and look after—work, family, hobbies, entertainment, the TV, the computer—that quality time in solitude and deep reflection has become rare. This constant busyness prevents us from having a deep relationship and connection with ourselves. And still, this is one of the most important and rewarding things we can do.

We don't need to go to a retreat center—although this is a marvelous thing to do from time to time—to be able to find quality time in solitude, in the company of ourselves. Opportunities exist during a walk in the park, a moment when we sit in our living room with the TV switched off after the rest of the family has gone to bed, a trip in our car when we switch off the radio and slow down, any occasion of solitude when we mindfully exercise the intention of being intimate with ourselves.

The key factor is the conscious intention of being with ourselves and reflecting on our Life—with a capital L. That means not just our preoccupations of the moment, but the deeper meaning of Life and its bigger picture. Our contemporary society seems to be built around preventing us from having this kind of deep reflection and connection. In fact, we have a whole media industry fighting for our attention, so if we want this deep connection in our own Lives, we need to seek it on purpose.

By developing this intimacy, a new kind of relationship with ourselves will arise, one based on respect and appreciation for the life that we have been given and for the living beings that we are. This single factor can change our whole life.

By pursuing these deep connections, we can satisfy our need for connection; heal feelings of loneliness, isolation, and alienation; and fill our hearts with aliveness and joy. It all comes down to our desire, intention, and willingness to connect; then our own hearts will help us by doing their own part. A little change can change it all.

CHAPTER EIGHT

Rekindle Your
Joie de Vivre

We are in the middle of our journey to a vibrant aliveness and have reached a very important step. So far, we have seen how to get our bodies vibrantly alive, how to enhance our life force, how to open the flow of feelings, and how to make our hearts more vibrantly alive through connection. Continuing with the heart's aliveness, now is the time to discuss filling it with joy.

Joy is a vibrant emotion that enlivens us at the heart level and that can come from different sources. We can experience joy when we achieve something we have worked hard for, like the day we get a university diploma, or a certain job, or that house we dreamed of. We can experience joy playing with our kids on a sunny afternoon in the garden. We can experience joy eating that food that we love so much. However, within the context of this book, I am going to address the filling of our hearts with joy through the broader perspective of our joy of living, or, as the French call it, our *joie de vivre*. This expression may be translated as both *joy of living* and *enjoyment of life*.

As we saw in chapter three, one of the characteristics of the Mediterranean spirit is the philosophy of enjoying life, this being a source of joy of living and aliveness for the Mediterranean cultures. We can experience an overall joy of living through the very fact of enjoying life.

I don't want to sound frivolous and to dismiss here the challenges that we face in our lives, or the important problems and struggles that some people experience that can significantly decrease their joy of living. Still, the way we face challenges makes a big difference in our ability to experience *joie de vivre*. There are people who have very little in material wealth, yet enjoy life very much. Others with serious handicaps or illnesses have a degree of joy of living that many others without their situations never manage to experience. So, showing my greatest respect for the challenges that we human beings sometimes have to face, I want to make the case here for *joie de vivre* and how it is more a function of how we live our lives and understand them than the circumstances we encounter.

Let's see a few ideas on how to increase our *joie de vivre* and fill our hearts—and our lives—with joy.

A question I often ask the participants of my programs is, "What is your happiness menu?" By this, I mean, "What are all the things that your life has to have in order to make it a delight for you to enjoy?"

I like to use the metaphor of a restaurant meal (I believe my Mediterranean Spanish background has something to do with this). Think of different kinds of food you love and really enjoy eating; then create what would be a really amazing dinner menu for you that would make that dinner a memorable experience of enjoyment and delight. What different dishes will be part of this menu?

If you take this experience to the wider context of your life, what are the different aspects of the experience of living that make—or could make—life a delight for you to enjoy? What experiences do you savor, do you really enjoy?

Notice that I use the words "experiences" and "savor" because enjoyment always comes from experiencing. Do you love the experience of being in nature? Do you love the vigor that comes from physical experiences, such as sports or other physical activities? Do you love the experience of connecting with others from the heart? Do you love the experience of spending time alone with a good book? Do you love the experience of playing or listening to music? Do you love the experience of cooking?

Ultimately, our lives are made of our experiences, and so too is our happiness. Sometimes we think that we will be happy when we have certain material things or achieve certain goals, only to realize when we get there that we don't feel the happiness we expected. Wants and goals are perfectly legitimate for us to pursue, and they can be a source of purpose, meaning, and enthusiasm that enlivens us at the soul level, and hence give us joy of living. The problem arises if, in the process of working on them, we lose our enjoyment of life.

A good exercise to help you gain clarity on your "happiness menu" is to set some time apart to meet with yourself in an intimate conversation to get clarity on this very important aspect. As we saw in the previous chapter, modern life tends to keep us from this kind of intimate contact and reflection, trying to convince us that happiness is in whatever is being promoted and marketed. In my programs, one of the things that people value the most is this opportunity to just take a little time to ponder and reflect on the important things of life.

As a guide for your reflection, consider the following questions.

- What are the aspects of the experience of being alive that make—or could make—your life a delight to savor?
- What do you love to experience?
- What makes you vibrant with energy?
- What fills you with happiness?
- What do you enjoy doing?

You already know about the things that make you happy or that you love. These questions are just a means to guide your reflection and bring them to the surface of your consciousness. In the additional resources of the book, you will find a chart you can use to create your "happiness menu" and a poster that will keep it very present in your daily life. In the Resources section at the back of the book, you will find how to get it.

When our lives contain those experiences that we love and enjoy, our joy of living naturally increases, as does the aliveness and vibrancy of our hearts, which, in turn, increases our joy of living in a sort of feedback loop.

Another thing that we can do to rekindle our *joie de vivre* is let little children become our teachers and guides.

In normal circumstances, children find life to be an endless stream of discoveries, an adventure, something to play with, something to enjoy. Of course, it helps that they don't have the responsibilities, challenges, and desires that we adults have, and children are discovering everything for the first time.

But would it be possible to recover and integrate into our adult lives some of those qualities that normally give children such *joie de vivre?* Yes, it is possible, and the key lies deep in our own psyches.

Psychologists have learned that our psyche is built around specific structures called archetypes, each of them being the carrier of different aspects or qualities of human experience. (I will discuss archetypes in more detail in the next chapter.) One of the structural archetypes that we all have is the one called the "child." This inner structure of us carries all the qualities that are so manifest when we are children: curiosity, playfulness, creativity, a sense of adventure, enthusiasm, wonder, spontaneity, and open emotion. When we were children, this structure was at the forefront, and with it were all these qualities. Then, in the process of growing up, we moved internally to other structures, losing a great many of these qualities, and with them, a great deal of the joy of living that they brought and that is so natural in children.

Our child archetype is different from our inner child. The archetype is, as its name reflects, archetypal; it contains the qualities of childhood, whereas our inner child carries our individual childhood experiences. I want to clarify this because for some people, their childhood was a difficult or even painful period of their lives. But the *child archetype* is the pristine child that comes into the world with every new baby.

What is important to know is that this part of us is still there. The child archetype didn't go away with our childhood, like our child body did; it just went to the background and can come to the surface. We can see this in moments when we get playful, spontaneous, loose, and creative. When this happens, our child has come to the surface, bringing with him or her the natural joy of living.

So, in rekindling our *joie de vivre*, we can call back our child into our lives. Does this mean we are to become childish? Not at all; it just means we are to access the childlike qualities of wonder, curiosity, and playfulness to refresh our lives and to create more joy of living.

How can we do it? By meeting our child in his or her natural realm: playful and creative activities. When we engage in activities that are playful and creative, our child archetype comes naturally to the forefront because playfulness and creativity are the natural land of the child.

There are different ways we can get playful and creative. We can go to the park to play with our kids, go out with friends to play ball just for fun, or get together with friends to cook a meal in a fun spirit. The options are endless, limited only by our imagination. The keys are the fun and play factors.

The expressive and creative arts are also a marvelous way to bring the child to the forefront. They have so much potential to transform our lives and to bring *joie de vivre* that can be hard to believe. Lucia Capacchione, in her book *Recovery of Your Inner Child,* puts it very clearly:

Creative activities done for the sheer joy of the experience (without pressure to perform) inevitably allow us to revive the Inner Artist that we lost in growing up. The enrichment of our lives that results from this bursting forth of the Creative Child is so far reaching as to be almost beyond words. You must experience it to believe it.

I would include in a list of such activities—those "done for the sheer joy of the experience"—the following.

- Dance
- Expressive movement
- Singing
- Voice expression
- Playing music
- Acting
- Improvisation
- Painting and drawing
- Molding and playing with clay

All these activities connect us with our sense of play, expression, easiness, creativity, spontaneity, joy, and imagination . . . the very qualities of our child archetype.

I can confirm this by my own experience and what I have seen in others. When I was attending classes in acting, contemporary dance, and singing, I felt so enlivened that they became a necessity for me. Since I engaged in them as a hobby, something that I did, as Lucia says, "for the sheer joy of the experience," I didn't have any pressure to perform, and hence I entered my playful and creative child state. These activities were so pleasurable and joyful that I never got tired of what I was doing. All my preoccupations, stress, and worries disappeared during these activities, and that real joy of being alive and playful carried over into my daily life. The time that I spent every week in these classes significantly increased my *joie de vivre* and helped me to face the responsibilities and challenges of my adult life with greater energy.

Creative expression is fun and makes us feel good about ourselves and about the world, which has a lot of power. It is not strange that today, these kinds of activities have become part of a therapeutic approach called art therapy that is showing to be very beneficial in the treatment of a varied range of psychological issues.

I find dance and expressive movement especially good because music is a wonderful vehicle for changing our mood, loosening us up, and putting us in a playful mode. Dance and expressive movement activities also provide room for playing with others. But this preference reflects my own love for music; maybe for you, acting or improvisation could be the perfect match.

Music and dance are very powerful ways to feel joyful and to get into expressive flow, which enhances our joyfulness. We can see this throughout history; music, dance, and singing have always been a way for human beings to celebrate the high points of life. I once met a Native American medicine woman who told me that since ancient times, in her tribe when people got sick and went to the shaman/healer for healing, the first things that they were asked by him or her were: "When did you stop singing? When did you stop dancing? When did you stop coming into the silence? When did you stop sharing with others?"

I think there is great wisdom in these four questions. The expression of feelings and vital energy through movement, dance, and singing is very healthy not only because it helps us to release pent-up energy and stress (which is behind most of our health problems), but also because the feeling of joy that these activities bring is profoundly healing.

Another way we can arouse our child archetype is through humor and laughter. We like to laugh but often forget to. The therapeutic approach called "laugh therapy" works with laughter and humor to bring the inner child forth. His or her careless, relaxed, and spontaneous ways are very therapeutic when we feel dull, dry, stressed, and grim.

Most of these creative activities are or can be social, meaning that they offer us the opportunity to be with and connect with others. As we have seen, this connection is another important source of joy and vibrancy for our hearts, and can be very healing for feelings of loneliness. A two-hour session a week in a playful, creative activity can literally change one's life for the better.

The "happiness menu" and the child archetype are two powerful means to bring joy into our lives and aliveness to our hearts.

With this step in our journey toward a vibrant aliveness, we leave the dimension of our hearts and get into the dimension of our souls and spirits.

CHAPTER NINE

Swim in Your Own River

I once heard a spiritual teacher say: "We all have our own river; we have to swim in our own river; if not, we will dry out." These words were said from a spiritual frame of understanding human life, the river being a metaphor for our own soul's purpose. This meaning requires, of course, that we believe in the spiritual dimension of life, in the soul, and in the spiritual purpose of our lives.

However, today, we have enough knowledge of the human psyche to understand the wisdom and the importance of this statement even without recourse to spiritual beliefs. In his studies of the depths of our psyches, Carl Jung, one of the most important figures in the field of analytical psychology, observed that deep in us, there are archetypal forces that push to be expressed in our actual lives. These forces are archetypal because they represent basic themes or character patterns that we humans can enact: the child, the father, the mother, the warrior, the sage, the artist, the princess, the teacher, the lover, the explorer, the creator, the dreamer, the hedonist, ... Jung called these patterns archetypes and found that they live within our soul and are behind some of our drives and motivations, in their quest to be expressed in our lives.

The archetypes have been known since ancient times, and we can find them in the mythologies of all cultures, one of the best known in the West being the Greek mythology, where the different gods and goddesses—Aphrodite, Apollo, Artemis, Ares, Dionysus, Hermes, Zeus—represent the perennial themes of the human soul's yearnings, imaginations, and desires.

Today, authors such as Caroline Myss teach archetypes from a more modern perspective. Myss talks about such archetypes as the *mother, father, knight, warrior, teacher, mystic, storyteller, hedonist, inventor, scientist, visionary, seeker, artist, healer, engineer, pioneer, explorer, entrepreneur, mentor, leader, and sage.*

This approach to archetypes, using more contemporary terminology, makes it easier for us to relate, compared with earlier approaches, such as Greek mythology.

What is important to know is that, although all the archetypes belong to the collective soul of humanity, and hence can be enacted by all of us, when it comes to our individual soul, some of them are much stronger than others. Looking at this from a spiritual frame of understanding, our personal archetypes, as Caroline Myss puts it, constitute what we could call the "personality" of our spirit and are related to our soul's purpose or destiny because by influencing our desires, motivations, and actions, they influence the direction and shape that our life takes. Nevertheless, if we look at archetypes from a psychological point of view, we can see them as deeper, unconscious structures of our personality that seek expression and that are behind some of our yearnings, motivations, and dreams. There is more to ourselves than our outer personality and conscious mind. Sigmund Freud, Carl Jung, and others gave us this insight from their empirical study of the human psyche, which coincides with the wisdom that we find in the different spiritual traditions.

Our personal archetypes, our inner personality, define the waters in which we are meant and called to swim, our own river. We may be meant to swim in the waters of artistry and creation, of mentorship, and of fatherhood, if these archetypes are part of our spirits. When we do it, and give expression to the facets of our spirits that our personal archetypes represent, we experience deep fulfillment and a sense of aliveness that comes from deep within, aliveness in the soul that comes from parts of our spirits coming to life.

As an example of how this works, I am going to use my own case.

Since very early in my childhood, I felt drawn to electronics. I loved to play with apparatus. When the technician came to our home to fix the TV, one of those first black-and-white TVs of the sixties that were built with valves, I literally couldn't take my nose out of that box when he opened it; it fascinated me. This motivation is what was behind my deciding to study telecommunications engineering. There is a part of me that loves mathematics and physics and the building of devices. The explanation for this can be found in my inner personality. Now I know that I have the archetype of the engineer; this is where my motivation came from, and this is why I enjoy working with physical devices.

Another archetype that I have is the entrepreneur. Business and companies have always appealed to me. In high school, I had my father buy me one of those home study courses on electronics. It was not only that I loved the topic; I dreamed of creating electronic apparatus and selling them. In college, together with other classmates, I started up a consultancy association to get projects in companies that would be done by the students. Later, in all my professional life, this drive to entrepreneurship has always accompanied me. When I give it expression, I notice I come alive. People even tell me that when I talk about dreams and projects, my eyes get bright and shiny.

There is also a mystic in me. This is where my appeal toward spiritual knowledge and experience comes from. Although this motivation began to manifest strongly in my thirties, I could see it already in my childhood and teenage years. I was, for instance, a devoted fan of the TV series *Kung Fu,* featuring David Carradine as a traveling Shaolin monk. I loved his interior life and mastery of both the interior and the martial art of kung fu. This is why, when I began learning about spirituality, consciousness, and the inner dimension of our lives, I felt I was swimming in my river; it was natural to me.

But sometimes an archetype remains dormant in our soul until something awakens it. This is what happened to me with the archetype of the artist. I was not aware of my artistic facet until I began doing activities like acting and modern dance. They opened to me a whole new world of experience that felt not only really good, but also natural to me. I began to realize how much I love aesthetic beauty, music, artistic expression, stories, and imagination. My engineer and my entrepreneur had been at the forefront of my life, driving the show, and not leaving much space for other facets of my spirit to come to life.

For me, the engineer, the entrepreneur, the mystic, and the artist are facets of my spirit that seek expression and the waters of experience in which I am meant to swim. When I give them expression and space in my life, I feel alive, joyful, and fulfilled.

Through our inner personality, we may be called to swim in the waters of art and music, or in the waters of helping others, or inventing things, or adventure, or leadership, or entrepreneurship, or motherhood, or fatherhood, or teaching . . . . Does this mean that if I am an engineer and have an artist archetype, I have to leave my work and pursue a career in the arts? Not necessarily. We can give expression to our archetypes in different ways within the frame of our present lives. If you want to leave your job as an engineer and pursue a career and the life of a musician, it is okay if you feel that inner drive, but you can introduce music into your life without having to make a major life change that you may not want, or be able, to make. By knowing our archetypes, we have powerful self-knowledge that helps us to make intelligent and informed decisions regarding our life.

Quite often, a lack of life satisfaction and vitality can be connected with our blocking the expression of the inner energies that pulsate in us and that seek to come to the surface of our lives.

There is a story about a surgeon who was very successful in his profession and his life but who, in his mid-fifties, began to notice deep in his heart a feeling of dissatisfaction and unfulfillment. Instead of neglecting it, he decided to give this feeling some space to be manifested and inform him what it was about. He set aside regular alone time, to be by himself, listening. As always happens when we listen, he began to receive the message behind that feeling. In his young years, he loved science fiction and wanted to write. He wanted to become a writer, but he decided to go into medicine, which he also loved, and built a career in it.

With this information, he made the decision to give some time to this longing of his heart. He organized his responsibilities so that he could have some time every week to engage in writing a science fiction novel. He not only found that he loved this time, but he also began to feel a stronger life satisfaction and sense of aliveness. Writing became part of his life, and after this first novel, he wrote others. Being a success story, it has to be said that the novels got published, and he eventually left his work as a surgeon to devote his days completely to his writing, the calling that was most urgent in his soul. Even if the novels had never gotten published, still it would be a success story because of the fulfillment and joy that he found in writing. One day, talking to his sons, he said to them, "It is very important to listen to your heart and not neglect it."

This is a good example of a person whose artist archetype, which had been dormant for a long time, awakened. Instead of burying its voice, he listened and found not only deep satisfaction, but also vibrancy and aliveness. In our times, we are so used to trying to find quick fixes to deep feelings that are uncomfortable that we tend to bury them instead of taking the time to listen to their message.

Independent of our being conscious of it or not, our archetypes are there, trying to be expressed in our lives. Their means of communication is our heart, and its vehicles our longings, motivations, deep desires, dreams, dissatisfaction, even depression. We can learn to cooperate with our spirit, with our inner self, by paying conscious attention to our heart and through seeking self-knowledge.

Knowing our inner self personality is one of the best things we can do, and it is not as difficult or mysterious as it can appear. It just requires our willingness and some inner listening and reflection to go quite far in this endeavor. The rewards are many.

We also can engage in more formal self-knowledge work through certain personal growth methodologies and approaches. As I said, I find that Caroline Myss's approach is very valuable and practical because it puts archetypes in modern terms and also because it can be used from both a spiritual understanding and a psychological one.

The key is to understand our archetypes as characters that live within us, our inner self personality being the sum total of them. The way to identify these characters is by looking at our heart and our life with the intention of finding our inner motivations and drives, and then matching them with a certain character.

Let's look at an example. If I have an inner drive to help people and to look after them, I feel motivated to do this, and when I do it, I feel very good and inspired. This is telling me that there is a caretaker within me. With this realization, I recognize a whole facet of my inner personality, and this is much more powerful than just knowing that I feel good helping people. We need to look at our motivations through the lenses of whole identities. If I understand that in me resides a caretaker, I can consciously seek ways to help this facet get expressed and realized.

Another example: All of our lives, we may have had the deep desire to start up our own businesses, not just for the sake of money, but for the sake of entrepreneurship. But things didn't turn out quite that way, and we have ended up having a job. This motivation speaks of the possibility of our having an entrepreneur living within us, an entrepreneur that is seeking realization. Well, entrepreneurship doesn't necessarily have to mean starting up our own business and making our living out of it. It can mean to start something up, to create something, to lead something—and the possibilities for this *something* are endless. If we stay with the desire, in this case, to start up a business, the possibilities are limited, and maybe the way we have structured our lives makes it very difficult or disrupting to attend this inner need, which we may not want, but if we look at this desire and motivation as belonging to our inner identity as entrepreneur, we can seek ways to introduce into our lives the creation of or the starting up or the leading of something, bringing with it deep inner satisfaction and aliveness into our lives.

I have developed the following exercise to help you reflect on your drives and motivations, and identify the facets of your inner self. Be aware that this is ongoing work; it is good that you do it several times and that you always keep an eye on your daily life to identify motivations that you could tie in with your inner archetypes.

Bear in mind that archetypes can activate throughout our lives and call for expression strongly at certain ages. What is important is that in the present, we serenely see what our deepest motivations and dreams are, which have been with us forever, which ones we have satisfied, and most importantly, which ones are calling for expression.

Exercise: My Inner Self Personality

The following questions will help you reflect upon your drives. When pondering them, focus on your heart, instead of your mind. For instance, you may have always wanted to have financial stability, but this can come from your mind, from what you have learned in your family, from what you have learned is good and desirable. These kinds of desires can be good—although others can be quite limiting—but what we are after here is the deep longings and motivations of your heart, so don't focus so much on your wants, but on what pulsates in your heart.

Set aside enough time alone to do this; you can take a whole morning or afternoon. If you have a family and it is difficult to do it at home, take a Saturday or Sunday morning to go alone to a place where you feel comfortable and serene, a place that helps you get introspective. Don't forget to bring a notebook with you to write down your reflections.

Then, looking at your life, past and present, ponder in your mind the questions. Give yourself enough time to let your heart activate with the question and your mind identify answers. Let each question sink deep in you, go beyond the surface and deep into your heart.

When answering the questions, keep in mind the perspective that we are not a single personality, but a panoply of sub-personalities that sometimes can seem incompatible with one another. Don't try to put logic in this; just look at your heart, and play with your imagination. For instance, in the first question, you could say that you would like to live the life of a family man/woman and the life of an adventurer. They seem very different and not very compatible with each other, but we are not looking for compatibility or logic, but for longings of your heart.

You may find that some of the questions seem the same. Still answer them because we are trying to approach the finding of your archetypes from different angles.

Questions for You to Ponder

- If you had unlimited time and could live as many kinds of lives as you wished, which ones would you choose? (Write at least three to five possible life scenarios.)
- If you could be in a movie, what characters would you love to play? (Write at least three to five.)

- Who are the people whose lives speak to you?
- Which things have you always felt drawn to do?
- What comes naturally to you?
- What experiences or places are especially inspiring to you?
- What are the things that, when you get engaged in doing them, cause you to lose track of time?
- What is now knocking on your door that you haven't quite given expression to?

With all the answers to the above questions at hand, can you come up with a list of the characters that live in you? You may have a politician, an artist, a businessman/woman, a teacher, a visionary, a hedonist . . . . Just play with identifying characters in you. Try to identify three to five.

- Do you feel these characters are natural facets of yourself?
- Are you giving expression to all of them?
- Which ones are under-expressed or not expressed at all in your life?

The information about our inner personality is very valuable because it gives us self-knowledge that will help us design our lives in a way that we feel fulfilled and alive. Remember, there are many creative ways to give expression to our archetypes without making a major disruption in our lives.

Giving expression to the fullness of your spirit will bring vibrancy to your soul and joy of being alive to your life. The great mythologist Joseph Campbell puts it so beautifully in his book *The Power of Myth:*

People say that what we're all seeking is a meaning for life. I don't think that's what we're really seeking. I think that what we're seeking is an experience of being alive, so that our life experiences on the purely physical plane will have resonances within our own innermost being and reality, so that we actually feel the rapture of being alive.

Our inner being is a reality that is there. Through their myths, ancient cultures acknowledged it and gave it its rightful space in their lives. However, in our modern world, so saturated with scientific and materialistic thought, this more subtle reality has lost much of its space in favor of more concrete realities, such as our outer personalities, our bodies, and our feelings. However, if we want to experience the rapture of being alive that Campbell mentions, we need our soul to be vibrantly alive.

The expression of our inner self—or, as Joseph Campbell puts it, the alignment of our life experiences with our innermost being—is a way to bring this vibrancy to our soul. However, there are more ways. In the next chapter, we are going to explore them.

Fill Your Life with Enthusiasm, Inspiration, and Meaning

For all the spiritual traditions, the soul is the part of our being that connects us with the ultimate source of life. All these traditions have something in common: the affirmation of the reality of a non-material realm of life that gives rise to all the material manifested universe, and that is its essence. From this basic common premise, every religion has developed its own set of beliefs, dogmas, and practices that in some cases have lost their deeper meaning and purpose. The word "religion" comes from the Latin verb *religare,* which means reunite—in this case, to reunite humanity with its source or creator. So, beyond the specifics of religion, we find the common ground of spirituality, a wider concept that points to the existence of the transcendent realm of life and ponders the connection we humans have with it.

In my own case, although I was born and raised within the Catholic tradition, I don't consider myself a follower of Catholicism or any other religion. Yet I am deeply spiritual in the sense that I believe that life is much more than the material level that we can see and touch, that there is a sort of creative principle, intelligence, or spirit that gives meaning, purpose, and direction to all that exists. As we have already seen, this principle takes many different names in the world religions—God, Tao, Krishna, Allah, Yahweh, Brahman, the Void—but in all of them, the essence is the same: the ultimate principle of life.

I have come to the conclusion that in the same way that some scientists of the last few centuries said that it made little sense to believe in God, today it makes little sense *not* to believe in the creative principle. Although science has yet to come forth with a theory that includes the spiritual realm, it has come far enough, especially quantum physics, to understand that the material level of reality is but a level, and that the deeper we go, the more materiality it loses and the closer we get to what spiritual traditions said based on the mystical experiences of their mystics and seers. Quantum physicists have found that, on a subatomic level, the physical universe is mostly made up of empty space, and that the principle of consciousness seems to be what gives rise to all that exists. I think this is important because our modern technological minds need to understand things rationally and are not so prone to blind belief.

In this last step, we are going to keep working on the vibrancy and aliveness of our souls—in this case, the vibrancy and aliveness that derives from alignment with this transcendent dimension of life. Let's do a little experiment to get started.

Remember a time in your life when you felt enthusiastic or inspired. How did that feel? Didn't you feel vibrant and alive deep inside?

Now remember a time in your life when you were doing something that meant a lot to you, that you deeply cared about, that made you feel a sense of purpose. How did that feel? Didn't you feel vibrant and alive deep inside?

I bet you did. This was so because enthusiasm, inspiration, and meaning animate the soul and fill it with life that comes from the deepest layer of existence. Look at the etymology of the words "enthusiasm" and "inspiration." "Enthusiasm" comes from *en theos,* which means "in God." "Inspiration" comes from roots meaning "in spirit." Both these words tell us that when we feel enthusiasm and inspiration, we are very connected with the higher source of life and hence our soul is highly vibrant and alive.

So, when we fill our lives with enthusiasm, inspiration, and meaning, we are actually enlivening ourselves at a very deep level. It is important that we seek these three inner states and set up our lives so that we experience them. It is true that our life challenges, responsibilities, or difficulties can take a toll on us, but it is no less true that we can come from inspiration and a deep sense of meaning when facing them.

Before continuing, I want to invite you to do a little exercise. Please do it; it will only take a few minutes, and it is important. Have with you a pen and a piece of paper.

Take a few deep breaths, and let yourself sink deeper and deeper within yourself with every exhale. Get into a relaxed and very present state. When you are in this state, write as many answers as possible to the following two questions. Don't think them through too much; let yourself get into a free flow.

- What makes you feel enthusiastic? What activities, projects, dreams, objectives, vision, . . . ? Remember that enthusiasm is a different inner state than joy; it is more about what excites and captivates you, about something you want to achieve or materialize.

- When do you feel inspired? In what moments, and while doing what, have you felt inspired, flowing, creative?

The answers to these questions are very important clues about what makes your soul come alive and aligns you with the transcendent and the deeper purpose of your life. Bear in mind that when we think about the deeper purpose of life, we tend to see it as a major mission or work that we have to do. Well, this can be so, but the purpose of each of our lives is something wider that includes certain experiences that we have to live. When we feel enthusiasm for something or are inspired by something, this is a clue that this *something* is aligned with our soul's purpose or with God's purpose in us, if you will.

If you feel a lack of enthusiasm and inspiration in your life, at the sight of the answers to the above questions, what could you add to your life experience to create more enthusiasm and inspiration? Think of it like an ingredient in a recipe; what specific activities, endeavors, or projects could you bring into your life that would give it more zest?

Bear in mind that these don't have to be big things that take a lot of time and energy from you that you may not have at the moment; little changes can produce incredible results. The extra soul energy that they will bring not only will make you feel very alive, but also will give you extra power and zest for your daily activities.

The third soul-igniting element is meaning. In his acclaimed book *Man's Search for Meaning*, Viktor Frankl, one of the icons of humanistic psychology, tells us of the human need for meaning. We need to see meaning in life and in our lives; it's very hard for us to live meaninglessly. Actually, depression very often can be tied to the loss of meaning and purpose in life. On the contrary, those who live meaningful and purposeful lives shine with aliveness.

We can find meaning and purpose in many aspects of life. The taking care of a family, the raising of kids, the pursuing of a professional career, the manifestation of our dreams, the mastering of something, the engagement in something or some cause we deeply care about, ... All these are ways to experience meaning and purpose *in* our lives because they all can give sense and a sense of direction *to* our lives. However, the need for purpose and meaning doesn't stop here.

Not long ago, I went to a bookstore and got into a conversation with the salesperson about self-help books and what people look for in them. He told me that one of the topics that people are seeking the most is the subject of meaning and purpose in life. This is confirmed by such polls as the World Values Survey of the University of Michigan, which states that more and more people think often about the meaning and purpose of their lives. This yearning for deeper meaning brings us directly to the realms of spirituality and the soul.

On a psychological level, we need purpose and meaning in our lives, but also on the soul level, we need alignment of our lives with their deeper meaning and purpose. This is where that yearning comes from and where inspiration and enthusiasm, apart from being very vibrant inner states, come to help. All spiritual traditions talk about our lives having spiritual meaning and purpose. Our thirst and longing of the heart for transcendental meaning and purpose can be the proof that this view is correct.

I invite you now to do another introspection exercise to go one step further in imbuing your life with meaning and purpose. When it comes to this, there is no other way than looking inside and listening because no one else can tell us the purpose of our lives. This is a responsibility that we can't and shouldn't pass on to others. This exercise can seem a little gloomy at first, but from this vantage point, the deepest longings of the heart can come to the surface.

Go and sit comfortably in a quiet place where you will not be disturbed for fifteen to thirty minutes. Then take a few deep breaths, and let your body get loose and your mind more and more relaxed; with each exhale, release tension, stress, and preoccupations, and get more and more into a relaxed serenity.

Close your eyes, and travel in your imagination to the last day of your life. Imagine that you have lived a long life, and the journey has come to its inevitable end; you are ready to leave; you feel peaceful, serene, and satisfied with the life you have lived. In that moment, you take a final look into what your life has been.

What would you want to see?

What would make you feel deeply satisfied about your life?

What would give your life meaning?

What would make your life matter?

What legacy do you want to leave in the world?

Since our families are normally a very important part of our lives and a source of meaning, when answering these questions, we tend to focus very much on them. If this has been the case with you, I encourage you to do the exercise again, but with a wider focus.

Answer the questions from the wider perspective of the journey of the soul that is in this life for a reason. Bear in mind that there are five areas of meaningful engagement with life:

- Ourselves
- Our families
- Our community
- The planet
- The transcendent

With ourselves, we can live purposefully in:

- Our own personal growth
- Our self-realization
- The materialization of our dreams and aspirations
- Our professional growth and career

With our families, we can live purposefully in:

- Their well-being and nurturing
- Love and deep connection with them
- Helping them in their growth and self-realization
- Helping them to have a joyful and rich life journey
- Helping them to realize their dreams and aspirations

With our community, which is the group of people we belong to, including our friends, our coworkers, our colleagues, and our neighbors, we can live purposefully in:

- Its well-being
- Its growth and positive transformation
- The bringing of joy and a positive impact

With the planet, we can engage in its well-being and the bringing forward of a new and better world.

- What would you like to see that is not here yet?
- How could you make a contribution to a better world for the next generations?

With the transcendent, we can live purposefully in:

- Our spiritual awakening
- Our alignment with its will

Meaning, enthusiasm, and inspiration, together with giving expression to the fullness of our spirit, fill our soul and our life with vibrancy and aliveness. But there is still one more thing we can do: make our life an interesting and exciting journey.

Have you ever gone on a journey? I am sure you have . . . maybe when you've gone on a trip to a foreign country, or when you've gone to spend the weekend in a place you wanted to explore, or when you've gone to an antiques market in the city and you were so interested in all those things you were seeing, or when you read a novel that you found so interesting you couldn't put the book away. How did you feel? Did you feel excitement? Expectation? A sense of adventure? Curiosity? Engagement? Fun? These are the kinds of feelings that journeys produce in us, and these feelings make us feel vibrantly alive. Why not live our life this way?

For some people, life is a journey of discovery, adventure, and opportunity to live experiences, to learn, to grow, to savor, to do meaningful things, whereas others have fallen prey to the routine and lost the excitement of discovering and experiencing life. The way we see our life makes a big difference in how we experience it. The reality we live in is eminently subjective and a function of the framework of understanding from which we look at it. If we decide life is a journey of learning, discovery, adventure, experiencing, and growing, it is, simply because we have decided to use a framework of understanding that is as valid as any other.

The more we live our life as a journey, the more it becomes filled with the above qualities. Is this approach compatible with our "down-to-earth" daily life? Yes, it is because beyond the specific circumstances, our life is what we make of it. For a little child, a visit to the park can be an amazing adventure of discovery; why can't a day be for us adults an adventure and a discovery too? It all depends on how we look at life and how we live it each day. It is true that our responsibilities, challenges, and problems can take a toll on this attitude, but it is no less true that we are the only ones responsible for how we experience our life. The external circumstances may not be under our control, but we are always, always the captains of our soul and of how we live, whatever circumstances we are in. As when we talked about *joie de vivre*, here again, little children become our guides because they are masters of the excitement of the adventure of life.

The fact is that our life is a journey and an adventure whether we look at it from an existential point of view or from a spiritual one. Wisdom traditions have always talked about life being a journey of the soul, a journey for the soul to grow, to experience, and to learn. So our deciding to see and live our life as such a journey can be a wise decision. Why not live life from this wider perspective and obtain the benefit of the enlivening this provides? Why let our daily routines and challenges shade the deeper meaning of our life and deaden our soul? Why not live the excitement, adventure, and wonder that we experience when we are little children and are so interested in discovering the world?

With this step, we have reached the final stage of the seven-step process that I have designed to help others be and feel vibrantly alive. We have journeyed through the lands of our bodies, our hearts, and our souls, seeing ideas and practical initiatives you can take to bring vibrancy and aliveness into your life, and as a natural consequence, joy of living, the joy of being alive.

If you have taken action while going through this journey, by now you must be experiencing the positive effects of it. If you decided to read the whole book before moving into the action part, I want to take the opportunity at this point to once again stress the importance of taking action to get results. It is only through action that results come. There is a wise saying that states, "Life helps those who help themselves."

In any process of personal change, there are challenges that we must face. Some of them come from our external circumstances, whereas others come from inside of us. In the next chapter, we are going to see the two most common inner challenges that we may have to face, and how to overcome them.

PART III

IGNITING
THE MOVE

CHAPTER ELEVEN

Overcoming the
Inner Obstacles

Have you ever tried to come to a complete stop, a state of complete stillness, from a full-speed sprint? I'm sure that, at least in your childhood, you did. What happened? Were you able to stop suddenly, or did it take two or three seconds and several steps to be able to do it?

This is called the law of motion (sometimes also referred to as inertia), and it is a law of the physical universe. Physical objects, our bodies being among them, tend to stay in the state they are in, be it stillness or movement, and it takes some kind of force and time to move from one state to the other.

This physical law also has a bearing on our psychology. We are beings of habit, and we tend to cling to the status quo, despite our contentment or discontentment with it. The force of habit exerts a pull on us and creates resistance to change. This is a challenge we face whenever we want to change something in our lives.

In addition to inertia and the force of habit, there is another challenge that we might have to face: our personal history.

The very fact that we are adults means that we have a personal history. We have gone through experiences that have left imprints on us, some of them empowering and expanding, but others disempowering and limiting. The latter can become a real obstacle to our efforts to improve our life experience and, therefore, needs to be addressed.

In this chapter, we are going to examine these two challenges and address ways to overcome them so that you can get stronger and quicker results in your being and feeling vibrantly alive.

Resistance to Change

Any change initiative needs extra energy to break the status quo and move to a different state. It is like with water; if we want to create steam from water, we must heat the water, to apply energy, so that it moves from the state of liquid to the state of gas. The substance remains the same, H_2O, but the state changes. The same principle applies with human beings; if we want to change something in our lives or ourselves, we need to infuse ourselves with extra energy to overcome the pull of habits and the status quo.

This extra energy comes from something very basic: making a decision. You need to make the decision to change the status quo you are in at the moment if you are to really change it. If you want to live a vibrant and joyful life, you need to decide that that's what your life is going to be. A decision is what will get you on the move and provide the extra energy required to counteract the force of habit and break the status quo.

But this that sounds so simple is not. Many people only move when they reach a point of being totally fed up with their life situation or face a personal crisis. This gives them the push to get into action and change things. But we can also make the decision out of desire.

Just remember when you've had a strong desire for something. Did you get into action to get what you wanted? Did you feel the pull of the desire? Did you do what it took? I bet you did. Desire is a source of energy that propels us forward and helps us to break the status quo in order to get what we desire.

Do you want to feel vibrantly alive, to experience joy of living and deep fulfillment? Really? How big is your desire? Are you willing to do what it takes? Are you willing to bear the "discomfort" of breaking the status quo? These questions are important because unless you have reached a point of crisis in your life or of being totally sick of your situation, it is your desire that will get you on the move to take initiatives that will bring this aliveness and this joy into your life, if this is something you want to advance on. (Otherwise, I believe that you wouldn't have picked up this book to read and come this far in the reading.)

Let's pause for a moment and do an experiment. Please do it. We are going to engage your imagination.

I want you to imagine yourself feeling vibrantly alive and joyful. Maybe you could draw on memories of the past when you have felt that way, but don't limit your thinking only to memories. Use your imagination. What is it like for you to be and feel vibrantly alive? See and feel yourself living a life in which you feel vibrant and very, very alive; see and feel yourself in different situations but in all of them feeling this aliveness. See and feel yourself feeling the rapture of being alive, as Joseph Campbell expressed it; how does this kind of rapture feel for you? See and feel yourself vividly; picture it in your imagination with as much vivid detail as possible. Feel it; feel it real. Stay there as long as you want, enjoying it. Then come back to the present time and moment.

Now go and do it. Close your eyes, take a few deep breaths, and get relaxed, loose, and centered within yourself; then go into the visualization. Enjoy it, and let yourself be imbued by the experience.

We've just done an imagination exercise to help you have a vivid experience of what we are after. I know it is not the same as the actual experience, but our imagination can help us a great deal to feed our desire; you already know this.

This image that you produced in your imagination is a powerful aid for you. On one hand, it ignites and feeds your desire, giving you energy and motivation to go for it. On the other hand, it informs your subconscious mind of the reality that you want to manifest, and by doing this, your subconscious will become an ally and help you manifest this reality. Bear in mind that in this universe, things are created twice: first in our minds, and then in the physical world, so if you want to be and feel vibrantly alive, you have to create that version of you in your mind first.

Once the image is created, the process of manifesting it in the real, physical world begins. For this, you need to nurture the image as you would a seed of a plant that you've put in soil and want to sprout and grow by watering it. You nurture the image and keep it alive in you by bringing it every day for a few minutes to your conscious mind and watering it with the energy of expectation, intention, and love.

By doing this, the new you will begin to breathe bit by bit, first in your mind, and from there in your reality. This is a very important ritual to keep; it only takes five minutes every day. You can do it at any time during the day, but in the morning, when you are ready to begin your day, is ideal and a perfect moment.

We are not talking about metaphysics here (well, maybe a little bit), but about keeping your objective very vivid in your mind, about nurturing your desire, and about facilitating getting yourself into action to manifest it. Also, this image will become a major force in your subconscious mind that will unleash all your potential and take you in the direction of manifesting it.

But don't forget, this is only one-half of the process; the second half is you moving into action by taking the initiatives we've seen in the previous section. With this strategy, results will come.

Don't get impatient; sometimes the seed takes its time sprouting and coming out of the soil. Just keep taking care of it, nurturing it, and putting into action the initiatives of the seven steps, and bit by bit, at your own natural rhythm, you will become more and more vibrantly alive and joyful. You even may be surprised at the speed the process takes at a certain moment. It always amazes me what happens with the bamboo seed. When you put it in the soil, it takes around seven years for it to sprout and give the first stalk—you may even think that nothing is happening, but this is the way the bamboo process is—then once this first stalk appears, in a very little time, the bamboo grows to an amazing size.

Feeding your desire and nurturing the image of the vibrantly alive and joyful you will help you overcome this first of the inner challenges: inertia. Now let's see how to overcome the second of the inner challenges.

Imprints from the Past

Another challenge in our journey to a vibrant aliveness is the effect of imprints from the past, one of the most common being feelings of insecurity and not being good enough.

It is important to understand that these kinds of feelings are quite universal and widespread. We may not feel good enough because our parents, in their desire to bring good to us, stressed our weaknesses too much and emphasized the need for improvement, or we may feel insecure because when we were in high school, we did not fit the model of beauty or athletic prowess that the media promoted. Perhaps these feelings got so entrenched in the core of our being that many years later, we still feel the echoes of them.

I have been privileged to sit all along my journey with many groups where sharing from the heart was encouraged, and I have noticed two things: First, when people open their hearts to go beyond the surface persona they present to the world and show their deepest feelings, issues of fear, shame, and insecurity tend to appear. Second, when in a safe atmosphere where people are able to open their hearts, they feel so good, not for the display factor itself, but for the experience of opening the heart and really connecting with their deep feelings, with their deepest self, which tends to be neglected in order to live in the world.

To be able to experience the vibrant aliveness we have been talking about, we need to feel good about ourselves. When deep inside we feel shame, insecurity, or "not good enough," our attempts and efforts to experience that vibrancy always end up hitting the wall of these deep negative feelings.

In some cases, our life experiences may have left us with traumas, emotional wounds, and deep issues that need the help of a professional therapist. However, the feelings of insecurity, of shame, and of not being good enough that so many people seem to carry, and that are very much connected to the way they have been raised and the biases of their culture, can very much be worked with on our own and healed by a treatment of unconditional love and unconditional acceptance of ourselves.

Love is a quality, an energy that makes us shine. When we are children, we shine when we are treated and cared for with love. We blossom as a flower before the loving eyes of our parents. There are even experiments done with plants that show how the ones cared for with love grow bigger, healthier, and brighter. Love is the primary nourishment that we need.

However, the supply of nurturing love in our childhood can get messed up with other aspects, such as behavior, expectations, mind-sets, and society models. All of them take a toll on our feeling unconditionally loved and accepted, and on us developing that same feeling for ourselves. Feelings of shame, of not being lovable, of not being acceptable or good enough can lie deep in our hearts and may be traced back to the way we were treated in our childhood. It is not that we have to blame our parents, relatives, educators, or childhood friends; normally they didn't know any better. This is part of how our society functions; it keeps telling us that we are not good enough, that we need to have that degree or education to be acceptable, or to drive that kind of car to be appealing to the other sex, or to wear certain brands of clothing to feel good.

But as adults, we have the possibility of revising all these messages and marketing ploys to free ourselves from their grip. There is nothing that prevents us from loving ourselves and accepting ourselves unconditionally. It is an inner decision independent of external conditions. Even if we don't feel good about certain things that we have done, we can always forgive ourselves and find reconciliation.

As adults, we have the opportunity to develop with ourselves the nurturing, caring, and loving relationship that we would have with a little child who needs our support to grow and blossom like a marvelous rose. As we have seen, that little child that we once were somehow still lives in us, and we have the opportunity to heal some of the wounds that she or he might carry by acknowledging our feelings and developing an unconditional acceptance and unconditional love relationship with ourselves.

When it comes to feelings of not being good enough—or intelligent enough, or attractive enough, or knowledgeable enough, or skilled enough—our real challenge is to question the belief that is behind these feelings; what does "enough" mean? How much is enough?

Bear in mind that we live in a media-dominated culture that creates heroes and heroines to generate revenue. This creates models of what is desirable that we absorb from the time we are little children, models that become part of our ideal self. To have ideals or seek excellence and improvement is not bad in itself, but problems arise when we lose ourselves—our own unique Self—and feel "less than" because we are not like the cultural models.

The truth is that from an existential and spiritual perspective, comparing ourselves with others and feeling bad because of it is the equivalent of a soul suicide. We need to see ourselves as a human life that is precious and important just because of the fact that it exists, like everybody else. When we see ourselves this way, we feel secure about our value, not putting it in relation to what others might be or have. We also feel secure about ourselves because we don't put this in the hands of circumstantial aspects; we feel secure about ourselves because we feel secure about our being, not about our skill set, knowledge, or possessions. All these things, by the way, can come and go. Our knowledge of today can be outdated tomorrow, especially with the fast pace of change we have nowadays. We can have a very good position in a company and tomorrow be made redundant, as has happened to so many people in the recent economic crisis. Or we can pass from having a good savings account to struggling to pay our mortgage. Self-security and self-worth based on external factors or comparisons are not built on solid ground.

Resistance to change and not feeling good about ourselves are the two most common inner challenges we have to face in any personal transformation process. When we have the energy to break from the status quo and we feel good within ourselves and deserving of the life that we want, we are halfway there.

To complete the journey, we just need a good strategy, and you already have that to advance in your own aliveness and experience the joy of being alive. Just refer back to the seven-step process seen in part two.

Passion for Life

o you feel passion for your life? Passion is a state of the heart that comes from our being in love. When we are in love with a person, passion is pulsating in our hearts. The same can be said when we are in love with something like the work we do, or music, or a sport we practice, or computers, or fashion, or anything that we love so much. Why not be in love with life itself?

Recently, I was walking in the park close to where I live, and I passed by the children's playground area. The energy emanating from these little ones was so vibrant that I couldn't help but sit on a bench and observe for a while. A little two-year-old boy was there playing in the sand and having the time of his life building small piles and then kicking them over with his feet, or taking a handful of sand and throwing it into the air, smelling it, literally dancing with that sand. He was absolutely excited by and interested in what he was living. Then I turned my attention to a group of five—three boys and two girls; they must have been around five years old. They were running around, chasing each other and shouting, "You won't catch me! You won't catch me!" But sometimes they got caught, and they squealed and laughed and tried to release themselves. It was so marvelous to see that display of vibrancy and life that for a few moments, I felt like going there and playing with them. But then I thought, *Well, I am a grown-up; what are all those parents going to think of me?* and discarded my inner impulse.

I have always loved to observe the passion for life that little infants have. They are so playful, enthusiastic, curious, and interested in discovering the world that it amazes me how, in the process of growing up, we tend to lose much of that passion for life. It is clear that our adult lives bring with them challenges that we don't have when we are children. We need to earn our living, we may have to face difficult situations, and, in general, we have to face pressures and struggles that belong to adulthood. It is not strange that our passion for life fades, in some cases nearly to extinction.

However, it is our passion for life that can bring us the ultimate joy of living. The more in love we are with someone or something, the more joyful we feel when we are with that person or doing that thing. With life, it is the same; the more in love we are with life, the more joy of living we experience.

Although I am not so prone to using religious quotations, something that Jesus once said comes to my mind: "I tell you the truth, unless you change and become like little children, you will never enter the kingdom of heaven." We can give this statement different meanings, one of them being that the joy that we associate with the idea of heaven comes from getting back some of the characteristics of childhood: openness, playfulness, enthusiasm, curiosity, and, ultimately, passion for life. Don't we feel we are in heaven when we are passionately in love with someone?

I believe that, along with the inner obstacles we saw in the previous chapter, rekindling our passion for life is another challenge we have on our way to a joyful life.

Is this an idealistic—and unrealistic—perspective of life? Not at all. This way of being in life doesn't mean we won't have challenges or difficulties because they are inherent aspects of life. Don't we experience challenges, too, when we are in love with someone? When we are in love with life, its challenges and difficulties don't impede us from feeling the passion for it because we live them from a different perspective and understanding; we never lose the wider view of the wonder, mystery, and adventure that life is.

As I am writing this book, my nephew has just turned one year old, and he is learning to walk. It is absolutely delightful to observe him in his struggles to get to the standing position, helping himself with a chair or whatever thing he can use to lean on. Every time he tries, it is so obvious by the expression on his face that he is struggling with the difficulty, but when he manages to get upright, a big smile comes over his face. We then get very happy with him, and when he sees our smiling and delighted faces at his achievement, he gets even happier.

It is true that sometimes life challenges us with difficulties, but it is also true that our attitude when facing them makes a big difference in the impact they have on our lives. I once attended a workshop where the therapist leading it worked with participants to help them understand the deep dynamics underneath some of their life struggles. At a certain point, he was working with a woman who was clearly suffering in her life, and he said to her—and to all of us, "In life, pain is unavoidable; suffering is optional." When I heard this statement, I thought, *He is so right.* Pain, challenges, and difficulties are part of life's journey, but the way we understand them and face them makes a big difference.

Falling in love with life is one of the best things that we can do, not just to boost our joy of living, but also to help us in facing whatever challenges we might have to face in our lives. We normally identify being in love with a certain "object," such as another person, our work or vocation, some activity we do, an area of knowledge, and so on. However, why not fall in love with life itself? Why not fall in love with the journey, experience, and adventure that life is?

Inviting as this question can be, there are two obstacles in our way.

On one hand, most of us are so immersed in our daily activities, responsibilities, and challenges that we rarely take the time to address the big questions of life: What is life about? What does it mean to be alive? Who am I? Why am I here?

However, these questions—and our answers to them—are precisely what give depth and meaning to our lives, and allow us the wider perspective that helps in being in love with life.

On the other hand, our past and some of the challenges and difficulties that we may be experiencing can take a toll on our passion for life. We may be in need of some healing.

If we want to be passionately in love with life, we need to water this passion every day. All the aliveness initiatives we saw in part two will nurture this passion because of the joy of living they bring. In addition to them, there is one more thing we can do: look at our life through the eyes of a lover. When we do this, passion becomes the base vibration of our hearts. But also, another interesting thing happens: The more we are in love with life, the more life will be in love with us, and we will enjoy all sorts of gifts from our lover—life itself. Is this a sort of metaphysical statement? Yes, it is, but metaphysics are real. Although they have not been the object of scientific study until recently, they are the land of wisdom acquired by humanity over thousands of years. And this wisdom says we attract what we emit. If we emit love, we attract love; if we emit hate, we attract hate; if we emit joy, we attract joy. We live in a mirror universe, where the outside mirrors the inside.

I believe that life is an amazing gift that we have been given. It doesn't matter what wider frame of understanding we use to give meaning to where our life comes from. For me, life is, ultimately, a mystery, a fascinating one, and a journey that I can enjoy, and in which I can play, discover, learn, and grow. And it is precisely the enjoyment, the learning, the growth, the play, and the mystery that makes me be passionately in love with life. Does this mean that my life is free of struggles and challenges? Not at all. I have my own share of these too, but my passion for life is stronger, a passion that I water every day looking at life through the eyes of a lover, never losing the wider perspective, and living from the aliveness principles we've seen in this book.

Epilogue

When I was planning to write this book, every time I mentioned the topic of aliveness to other people, I noticed them light up; their eyes would get shiny, and their voices became vibrant with excitement. I would say, "I am going to write a book on aliveness," and, in turn, they would become so enthusiastic and encouraging. Their response to the idea demonstrated that some deep longing in them was being touched.

It is true that happiness and joy of living are what most, if not all, of us ultimately want in our lives. Not in vain, Aristotle, the great Greek philosopher, defined "happiness" as "the ultimate goal that we pursue in all acts of our life." However, it is my belief—and this response of people to the idea of this book may prove it right— that what we ultimately long for is to feel vibrant and alive. Actually, as we've seen throughout the pages of this book, it is this vibrant aliveness that mostly gives us the joy of living that we seek.

We live in a time in history when material conditions, especially in developed countries, have reached a point where the pursuit of joy of living, that joy of living that I believe is our birthright, has become more possible than ever before. The advances in health, education, security, civil rights, and comfort of living have created a level of well-being that our predecessors in the line of human history didn't enjoy. Now we have the conditions that support the seeking of fuller and more joyful life experiences.

In this book, I have presented a way to fulfill this desire, the way of vibrant aliveness. It also could be called the way of vitality, joy, passion, love, enthusiasm, and self-realization, but as you've seen, all of these are encompassed in what I call a *vibrant aliveness.*

My personal journey gave me a deeper understanding of human nature, but most importantly, it ignited my passion for contributing to the aliveness and joy of living of others. Little did I know when I was studying telecommunications engineering and wanted to become a successful businessman that my life was going to turn out the way it did. But deep in my heart, I feel that it turned out the right way because when I think of this mission that I have given to myself, my heart gets so full and vibrant that I wonder if I am doing this for others or for myself. The truth is that in all these years since life took me out of my executive career, I have gradually opened up and found myself and my own way. I still have the entrepreneurial inclination I have always had, but now there is a meaning, a caring for others associated with it; it's not just about me.

I believe that each one of us has a contribution to make to the world. Even though we have our own individuality, we also are part of the wider whole of life and have our own share in its well-being. It is much like a human body. I've always been amazed at how this complex whole, composed of billions of cells, works in such perfect harmony to keep us alive. The only means for this is that every single cell makes its own contribution to keep the whole healthy, growing, and alive. Translating this into human terms, our contribution to the wholeness of life, to the world, if you will, has to do with our own gifts, talents, knowledge, and wisdom.

In my own case, my contribution could be none other than aliveness and joy of living. This is my passion, but this is also the wisdom I have acquired throughout my journey and, no less importantly, through my cultural DNA.

I believe that like each person, each culture has a gift and wisdom to offer to the well-being of the whole. In the case of the Mediterranean cultures, this gift has to do with aliveness and joy of living, and with this book, it is my intention to pass on to other people in the world a piece of this wisdom from which they can benefit.

That day I was at the retreat center in Canada, meditating and asking my inner wisdom for guidance, I came in with the vision of creating beautiful resorts for people to experience aliveness and the joy of living, and to acquire wisdom and knowledge that can help them in living joyful, fulfilling, and meaningful lives. I still have this vision. But the guidance I received turned out to be the writing of this book, and I wholeheartedly jumped into it, once again jumping into the unknown.

It seemed a natural step to share with others through a book what I had learned, the insights I had gained, and to help them through the power of the written word. And the result is the book you've just read. The writing of it has been a whole journey for me. It has pushed me to my limits; it has obliged me to clarify my ideas, and I have struggled along the way. But now that I am closing it, I feel the satisfaction of the work done. I believe it can be of help to others in advancing in their own happiness and joy of living.

I was once with one of my teachers having a conversation about life and happiness. At a certain point, he pointed to the window of the room in which we were sitting and said: "You see all this? (From that window, we could see buildings, the streets, cars passing by, and shops.) All of it has been built by people trying to find happiness, many of whom never achieved it." I was struck by the strong statement, but upon further consideration, I thought he was right. Happiness sometimes seems so elusive in the midst of life's challenges and difficulties. However, as Aristotle put it, it also seems to be behind all acts of our lives.

I don't see happiness as a state of complete satisfaction of all the desires we may have, whose list may be endless, but as experiencing the joy of being alive. The vibrant aliveness concept and ideas we've seen in this book have the power to bring this joy. My own experience, and what I've seen in others, tells me so, but so does the broader wisdom of the Mediterranean cultures.

Helping others in experiencing this joy of being alive is the contribution I want to make to the well-being of the whole and the mission I have set up for myself. I don't know if I have chosen this path or if it has chosen me. Life is such a mystery that we never know why and how things happen. But I do know that I am on the right path.

As the moment has come to give closure to this book, I have a single desire in my heart: that it can help you experience the joy of being alive.

Acknowledgments

Writing this book has given me the opportunity to review my whole life and realize how many people have contributed to it. I am deeply grateful to all of them, especially to my family, whose unconditional love and support have always been there, providing me with the strength to jump into the unknown and learn what I've shared in this book. This book is dedicated to them.

Thanks go to all the people I've met in the personal growth workshops I have attended. Their sharing from the heart taught me much more than the books I've read. Their generosity in sharing themselves melted my heart and made me open mine. Special thanks go to my gestalt training group: Mar, Vicente, Mónica, Elisa, Rosa, Cristina, Noelia, Juan Luis, Raúl, Miguel, Mario, Isabel, Pancho, Jorge, and Ana.

Thanks also go to the founders and staff of Findhorn, Esalen Institute, Omega Institute, Estudio 3, and Ciparh. Your commitment to help others grow and find their light is just priceless.

Thanks go to all the teachers whose books I've read or whose workshops I have attended, especially to Claudio Naranjo, Paco Peñarrubia and the Ciparh team, Fritz Perls, Caroline Myss, Deepak Chopra, Eckhart Tolle, Viktor Frankl, Allan Watts, Stanislav Grof, Peter Russell, Daniel Goleman, Arnold Mindell, Hellen Palmer, Robert Johnson, and so many others who, through their books, shared the wisdom they acquired over a lifetime.

Thanks go to all the friends who generously read the first manuscript and gave me feedback to improve it: Helga Tilden, Dale Taylor, Lisa Caruso, Jules Trocchi, Elaine Hodson, Yossi Yassour, and Christine Lines.

Special thanks go to Elaine Hodson for her generosity and support throughout the months that led to the writing of this book and for her encouragement to write it.

Thanks go to Mary Langford, who helped me get started with the project of this book, and to my editors Jeanne McCafferty and Amanda Rooker for their contribution toward organizing the material and giving the book its actual form.

Thanks go to Morgan James Publishing for believing in this book and deciding to publish it. I will always be thankful to you.

And finally, I want to give my gratitude to life itself for inviting me to get off of the life path I had decided to follow, and for the new realms of experience and knowledge that I found afterward and that taught me the real meaning of being alive and the joy of being fully alive.

About the Author

Juan M. Martín Menéndez is an author, speaker, and entrepreneur. At the age of thirty-six, life invited him into an adventure of personal discovery and transformation. The loss of his fancy job as chief executive officer for Spain and Portugal of a multinational technology company became a turning point in his life—and the beginning of a journey where he discovered truths about life that his telecommunications engineering studies in the university and management in business school had never taught him. Through a series of experiences, step by step, stage by stage, he discovered what he already knew in his Mediterranean heart: that the happiness and joy of living that we all seek has its roots in our being and feeling vibrantly alive more than in anything else.

Today he is on a mission to help others live vibrant and joyful lives through his speeches, programs, and various initiatives.

Resources

Throughout the book, I have mentioned the availability of additional material that you can use to work with this book, including the following:

- Mediterranean diet chart and tips

- Meditation exercise

- Yoga and body work modalities

- Happiness Menu chart

This material is free and available at the book's website. Go to the following address to download it: **www.thealivenessfactorbook. com/additionalresources**.

As a companion to this book, I have also designed an online program to help my readers get results and advance in their own aliveness and joy of living. I have written this book with the intention of providing you, the reader, with practical information that you can use to advance in this direction. However, from my experience, both in my own journey and in working with others, I know that when we get engaged in a process where we are guided and have support, we do really get results—faster.

If you are interested in knowing more about this program, you can see all its details at the following address: **www. thealivenessfactorbook.com/vibrantalivenessprogram**.

I also produce an e-newsletter, where I publish additional content, ideas, and resources to help my readers live vibrant and joyful lives. I'd love to have you join me. You can sign up to receive it at the book's website: **www.thealivenessfactorbook.com**.

Thank you for letting me be a part of your life's journey.

To your aliveness,

JMM

CPSIA information can be obtained at www.ICGtesting.com
Printed in the USA
LVOW12*0816180214

374168LV00007B/77/P